EXECUTIVE TRANSITIONS
in Student Affairs

NASPA
Student Affairs Administrators
in Higher Education

EXECUTIVE TRANSITIONS
in Student Affairs

A Guide to Getting Started
as the Vice President

Ainsley Carry, Editor

Foreword by Kevin Kruger

NASPA
Student Affairs Administrators
in Higher Education

Executive Transitions in Student Affairs: A Guide to Getting Started as the Vice President

Published by
NASPA–Student Affairs Administrators in Higher Education
111 K Street, NE
10th Floor
Washington, DC 20002
www.naspa.org

Additional copies may be purchased by contacting the NASPA publications department at 202-265-7500 or visiting http://bookstore.naspa.org.

NASPA does not discriminate on the basis of race, color, national origin, religion, sex, age, gender identity, gender expression, affectional or sexual orientation, or disability in any of its policies, programs, and services.

Library of Congress Cataloging-in-Publication Data

Executive transitions in student affairs : a guide to getting started as the vice president / Ainsley Carry, editor.
    p. cm.
 ISBN 978-0-931654-87-9
 1. Student affairs administrators--United States. 2. Student affairs services--United States--Administration. 3. Organizational effectiveness--United States. I. Carry, Ainsley.
 LB2342.92.E95 2013
 378.1'60973--dc23
                        2013042049

Printed and bound in the United States of America
FIRST EDITION

CONTENTS

PART II: *Transition Stories*

Foreword

There is wide agreement among leaders in higher education that colleges and universities are facing a period of unprecedented change, which threatens the very future of the American higher education system. It is equally clear that navigating the coming challenges will require strong and visionary institutional leadership. This book could not come at a better time as strong institutional leadership from chief student affairs officers (CSAOs) is critical to the future of higher education.

Colleges and universities are under increased scrutiny in key areas such as college completion, progress and persistence, gainful employment outcomes, and the development of employer-valued skills. Student affairs leaders and their staff will play essential roles in developing evidence-based programs that underscore the role of student affairs in these areas.

The CSAO role has become increasingly complex and politically nuanced, requiring a distinct combination of knowledge and instinct. In the last 5 years alone, the role has evolved to oversee an ever-widening list of challenges, including, but not limited to, the following:

- Managing Title IX *Dear Colleague* letter requirements, including changes to policies and judicial strategies.
- Exploring new ideas for managing career services, counseling centers, and health centers in response to changes in the funding models for higher education and student affairs.
- Complying with performance/outcome-based funding legislation in an increasing number of states.
- Managing presidential and provost transitions.
- Handling parent relations and issues of parental notification under a range of circumstances, including when students are

involved in alcohol-related incidents, attempted suicides, and mental health transports to local hospitals.

- Creating inclusive communities and encouraging civility on and off campus.
- Interpreting implications of the Affordable Care Act on student health services.
- Implementing new Office for Civil Rights Americans with Disabilities Act regulations related to the use of "threat to self" as a basis for psychological withdrawal.
- Responding to continued increases in mental health issues and cases of suicide ideation.
- Overseeing behavioral assessment/intervention teams and the increased role of case management in the student affairs portfolio.
- Developing meaningful assessment strategies.

Successful executive transition requires an expertise in these areas as well as a sound organizational leadership strategy that positions the student affairs division effectively within the institution. As Fred E. Fiedler and Martin M. Chemers (1984) wrote in *Improving Leadership Effectiveness,* "The quality of leadership, more than any other single factor, determines the success or failure of an organization" (p. 3). The success of any student affairs division is inextricably linked to the ability of the CSAO to effectively manage up and down the organization. Fiedler, who spent a large part of his career studying the personalities and characteristics of leaders, is known for his contingency model of leadership, which asserts that variables related to the environment often determine the style of leadership that is best suited to the situation. In other words, there is no one best way to lead.

Executive Transitions in Student Affairs: A Guide to Getting Started as the Vice President approaches the move to an executive-level position from just that standpoint: There are many ways to lead and manage successfully. At the same time, student affairs professionals looking to move into executive positions in the months or years to come must develop thoughtful plans for completing goals and objectives and begin building relationships well in advance of the first day on the job. Within the pages of this book, readers will find a rich sampling of experiences and insights offered by CSAOs who have successfully made the transition and continue to achieve long-term success in their respective organizations. While the book is targeted to aspiring and new vice presidents, current CSAOs looking to make another career move or working with a new president or provost will find the strategies and advice helpful as well.

Ainsley Carry has done a superb job of assembling a group of CSAOs who share their varied experiences in managing the executive transition and maximizing the opportunities that come with a new executive-level position. The case study approach employed in the second half of the book makes the reader pause and consider how to handle the most diffi-cult transition situations. Climbing the career ladder in student affairs requires a number of transitions, but few are as important as the transition to an executive-level post. With this book in hand, senior staff members can help ensure a smooth transition to a cabinet-level position and lay the groundwork for reaching their department's and institution's long-term goals and objectives.

Kevin Kruger
President
NASPA–Student Affairs Administrators in Higher Education

Reference

Fiedler, F. E., & Chemers, M. M. (1984). *Improving leadership effectiveness: The leader match concept* (2nd ed.). New York, NY: Wiley.

Introduction

Ainsley Carry

I have been fortunate to have moved through my career assisted by people who supplied advice and lessons at opportune times. Teachers, guidance counselors, coaches, parents, friends, and mentors shared words of wisdom that pointed me in the right direction. I received advice that was not always what I wanted to hear, but it always ended up being exactly what I needed. Throughout my career, I interacted with many people who offered support, assisted with interview preparation, gave advice for salary negotiations, and shared tips for jumpstarting my first year. For example, months before my first day as vice president for student affairs at Auburn University, I interviewed six active vice presidents to ask their advice about what I should focus on during my first year. I hoped for some guidence that could help me avoid terminal mistakes in the transition period. What I got from them became my roadmap for my first year as vice president.

Going through my first year, I learned much through mistakes I made myself and mistakes I saw other administrators make. I observed competent leaders fail miserably in their transition to a new institution. In one case, a new vice president was asked to step down after less than 2 years on the job. Every month I read about college presidents being asked by boards to step down after only a few years in the position. It made me wonder how someone who demonstrated mastery in a position at a previous institution could fail so miserably in a new setting.

Business articles on executive transitions at for-profit companies often highlight the attention these companies pay to bringing new executives up to speed on critical issues and challenges. However, this is not mirrored in higher education administration. Complications and challenges in the two fields are similar (e.g., personnel, finances, customer satisfaction, community relations, product and service delivery), but the methods used to prepare executives are vastly different. There is a gap in how educational executives are prepared for the transition compared with their corporate counterparts. The idea for this book was born out of this realization. How can we apply best practices in business to prepare senior administrators for executive transitions in higher education? The focus in this volume is on vice presidents for student affairs; future publications might focus on academic deans, provosts, and presidents.

Mission

The executive transition period—the time from job interview to the point of making consistently positive contributions in the position—is filled with opportunities and risks for newcomers (Watkins, 2003). New executives have a chance to start with a clean slate, avoid mistakes made by their predecessors, and see existing problems from a new perspective. However, they also face risks associated with being new: not knowing the culture and language, inability to distinguish allies from enemies, and lack of familiarity with landmines and sacred cows. In for-profit companies, researchers estimate that between 40% and 50% of new executives resign or are terminated after less than 2 years in the position; the majority of these failures are due to misunderstanding the leadership demands of the new situation (McCall & Lombardo, 1983; Wheeler, 2008). It is essential that new vice presidents for student affairs understand the most critical priorities in the transition period. Failure to do so can lead to wasted time and early failure in the new position.

The mission of this publication is to shed light on the opportunities and risks of transitioning into a vice president for student affairs position. In this volume, sitting vice presidents share strategies for transition success. Maximizing opportunities and minimizing risks are the primary tasks of the transition period for new vice presidents, and there are many ways to accomplish these objectives. Most vice presidents learned from their own mistakes; we hope to help readers minimize mistakes by sharing advice from those who have traveled the path. Chapters on specific transition topics—communication, culture, onboarding yourself, strategies for success, pitfalls to avoid, and making internal transitions—contain important lessons. Several chapters are written in a case study format to combine theory with context. We hope this information helps new and aspiring vice presidents avoid mistakes and excel in their transitions.

Target Audiences

This book is written primarily for aspiring and new vice presidents for student affairs. The contributing authors address issues aspiring vice presidents should be thinking about and the challenges faced by new vice presidents. We consider new vice presidents for student affairs who are interested in the perspectives of sitting vice presidents on questions such as "I just accepted the vice presidency; what should I do first?" "How do I build a 100-day plan?" "What should I be reading to get ready?" This book is also intended for anyone still in the transition period (the first 2–3 years) of a vice presidency. We think it will be a must-read addition to the curricula of institutes and workshops for new and aspiring vice presidents for student affairs.

Secondary audiences include active vice presidents for student affairs and graduate students in higher education administration programs. Active vice presidents for student affairs will find the text useful in making a transition to another vice presidency or reflecting on their own transition challenges. No matter how long a person has served as a vice president, transitioning to this position at a new institution is never the same, and the dynamics of every transition are unique; assuming you know everything can lead to problems. Graduate students in higher education administration programs can use this text to better understand the complexity of the role of vice president for student affairs as they consider their own career paths.

The issue of executive transition is pertinent in all fields: business, education, sports, health care, military, and manufacturing, to name a few. Everywhere that new executives have to transition into a leadership position, figure things out, and provide leadership, they face the complications of adjusting and negotiating success. This is true for all executive positions in the academic institution: the president, provost, vice presidents, and deans all face complicated transition dynamics that are unique and inherent to their jobs. This book is focused on the role of vice president for student affairs, but a similar book could be written for every executive position in higher education.

Approach

With assistance from the National Association of Student Personnel Administrators, vice presidents for student affairs were invited to write a chapter or respond to a case scenario. Participants came from all types of institutions: public, private, small, large, 2-year, and 4-year. Authors were asked to "reflect back on your transitions into the role of vice president. What did you wish you had been told before you started your first year? What advice did you wish you had received when you were aspiring to a vice presidency or taking on the new role?"

This book is divided into two sections. Part I contains seven chapters on specific topics written by 11 vice presidents. Part II contains five case scenarios with advice and responses written by 13 additional vice presidents. The two parts together offer an in-depth view of transition issues as well as practical advice for managing difficult situations. This compilation of perspectives (student affairs professionals from different institution types) and methods (full chapters and case studies) offers readers a broad spectrum of viewpoints and issues to consider when making the transition to the vice president for student affairs position.

Part I: Transition Essentials

The first seven chapters are written on specific topics related to executive transitions in college administration. The authors determined these topics—onboarding yourself, communicating with others, assessing and adapting to the culture, and having a strategy—were among the most essential matters for new vice presidents in transition. In Chapter 1 ("The Case for Executive Transition Education in Student

Affairs"), Ainsley Carry and Kurt Keppler argue why the subject of executive transition education in student affairs is important. In Chapter 2 ("Onboard Yourself"), Carry advises new vice presidents for student affairs to prepare themselves rather than wait for their new institution to get them ready for the job. In the best case scenario, employers will outline a comprehensive onboarding curriculum for new executives, but that is unlikely to happen in most cases. In Chapter 3 ("Cultural Challenges"), Brian Hemphill, Melanie Tucker, John Jones, and Susan Gardner highlight the need for new vice presidents to pay attention to culture. Adjusting to a new culture is often the steepest part of the learning curve, and neglecting to make the cultural transition can trigger an early departure. In Chapter 4 ("Making the Internal Transition"), Karen Warren Coleman shares her own story. Being the internal candidate holds a significant amount of risk, because failure could mean having to find another job. In Chapter 5 ("Communication"), Gage Paine notes that a communication plan is often not included in a transition plan to a vice presidency. Communication is one of the most important factors for a successful transition, yet it is often the most neglected aspect. In Chapter 6 ("Strategies for Success and Pitfalls to Avoid"), John Laws shares a number of commonsense but often overlooked strategies for success and perils to avoid in the transition. In Chapter 7 ("Assessing Campus and Divisional Cultures"), Houston Dougharty and JoNes VanHecke offer advice on how to assess the culture of a division and an institution. For external hires, cultural assessment can be the biggest transition hurdle; a sound approach to assessing culture is an important tool for a new vice president.

Part II: Transition Stories

Chapters 8 through 12 are case study scenarios that include responses from active and retired vice presidents for student affairs. The responses offer readers multiple—sometimes conflicting—options. Few challenges in executive transitions lend themselves to a single correct answer; in a case study, readers are exposed to different ways of thinking about and resolving a challenge. None of the responses to the scenarios is more correct than another; together, they offer an array of options. What matters most in resolving executive transition issues is the context of the problem (e.g., history, executive leadership culture, authority of the position) and the experience of the new vice president. Career experiences will help new vice presidents gauge the extent to which they can push or pull in resolving transition challenges. Readers are encouraged to come to their own conclusions about which pieces of advice are best for their own situations.

The five case studies are based on true stories of dilemmas faced by vice presidents for student affairs in transition. The names of participants and institutions have been changed to protect their identities. Each scenario is followed by advice from three to five active or retired vice presidents. In Chapter 8 ("Bait and Switch"), Andy Carr accepts a vice presidency that looks robust on paper. Upon his arrival, he finds that the position description was greatly exaggerated to attract candidates; in fact, more than half the departments listed actually report to the provost. What should he do? In Chapter 9 ("The Internal Candidate"), new vice president for student affairs Patricia Thompson faces a situation in which a senior member of her team was an internal candidate for the position. He is determined to disrupt her efforts to advance the division and plans to try to make her appear incompetent. How should Thompson handle this situation? In Chapter 10 ("A Bold New Vision But Declining Resources"), new vice president for student affairs Dan Marin is charged by the president to "pursue a bold new vision for student affairs." Toward the end of the planning process, the university suffers several major budget cuts and Marin has to revise the plan several times; the confidence of his leadership team wanes as the future grows increasingly unclear. How does Marin convince his team to move forward in the face of declining resources and uncertainty about the future? In Chapter 11 ("Crisis Response Protocol"), new vice president for student affairs Martha Jenkins begins her tenure with a focus on establishing a much-needed strategic plan for the division. Within the first year, her efforts are upended by two events that reveal deficiencies in the division's crisis response protocol. How should Jenkins decide what to focus on when there are so many competing deficiencies? In Chapter 12 ("Your Boss Is Your Predecessor"), new vice president for student affairs Carlos Santiago reports to the president of the university, who is the former vice president for student affairs. The president has not totally vacated the position: He often makes student affairs decisions without keeping Santiago in the loop, and Santiago does not have full rein to make decisions. What should he do?

Terminology

Higher education is filled with acronyms and terminology that vary from institution to institution. For consistency and to reduce confusion, we have attempted to standardize some of the terms. Authors were asked to use the same terms regardless of what positions are called at their institutions. Readers should translate these terms, where necessary, to apply to their particular situations.

- The title *vice president for student affairs* is used throughout to represent the highest ranking student affairs position. This position is also called, for example, dean of students, chief student affairs officer, vice president for campus life, or vice president for student services.
- The vice president for student affairs reports to either the president or the provost; some authors refer to this position as *supervisor* of the vice president for student affairs.
- *Executive* typically describes a corporate leader. It is used in some chapters to refer to educational executive positions such as president, vice president, provost, and dean.

Chapter Summaries

Each chapter ends with a summary of its major ideas and themes. These summaries are chock full of good advice for vice presidents in transition. Use them to preview a chapter before you read it, to identify specific topics for exploration, or to customize your own transition plan.

References

McCall, M. W., Jr., & Lombardo, M. M. (1983). *Off the track: Why and how successful executives get derailed* (Technical Report No. 21). Center for Creative Leadership, Greensboro, NC.

Watkins, M. (2003). *The first 90 days: Critical success strategies for new leaders at all levels*. Boston, MA: Harvard Business Review Press.

Wheeler, P. (2008). *Executive transitions market study: Summary report 2008*. Atlanta, GA: Alexcel Group and Institute of Executive Development.

PART I

Transition Essentials

.

CHAPTER 1

The Case for Executive Transition Education in Student Affairs

Ainsley Carry and Kurt Keppler

Every year, hundreds of educational administrators transition into executive leadership roles such as president, provost, vice president, and dean. They advance from assistant and associate ranks to the chief position. Some sail through the transition period, while others stumble or even are dismissed because they could not successfully navigate the transition. The authors review executive transition literature as well as the results of a survey of aspiring and active vice presidents for student affairs. This chapter highlights the need for educational programs for transitioning executives to help them avoid the pitfalls of the transition and succeed in their new positions.

The first year of any significant life transition is the most difficult. The first year is when the personal, psychological, and social adjustments are hardest to make. The first year of college, marriage, professional school, or moving to a new town requires the most adjustment. In the workforce, success in the first year is an important barometer of long-term success, because newcomers build confidence and trust—essential building blocks for performance—and develop survival strategies for navigating in the new environment. On the other hand, failure in the first year is detrimental to long-term success, because those who stumble lose confidence and have a difficult time rebuilding their brand. Stumbling in the first year of an executive position is especially damaging because of the high profile of these positions.

The first part of this chapter summarizes past research related to executive transition. The middle portion addresses transition issues related to higher education, specifically to chief student affairs positions. The chapter concludes with a discussion of a recent study of professionals who aspire to be chief student affairs officers (e.g., vice chancellors and vice presidents) and compares survey data on these individuals with opinions of sitting vice presidents on the same issues.

The Executive Transition Period

Every year thousands of executives in business and education advance to higher level leadership positions; retirements, promotions, and terminations open opportunities for advancement. Business executives—chief executive officers, chief financial officers, chief marketing officers, chief operating officers, and others—step into new leadership roles with high expectations from others and themselves. However, studies show more than 50% of new executives are terminated or resign within the first 18 months, and the majority will fail owing to lack of leadership/management skills, not of technical competency (McCall & Lombardo, 1983; Wheeler, 2008). Similarly, hundreds of new educational executives—presidents, provosts, vice presidents, and deans—step into executive roles for the first time and face challenges that cause many of them to succumb during the transition period. Similarities between executive transitions in business and education offer an opportunity to apply what has been learned in one field to practice in another. Too often, lessons learned in business are ignored in education.

Promotions, demotions, and terminations happen daily to millions of working people around the world. Employees can be demoted or terminated for a number of reasons, including poor work performance or conduct detrimental to the organization. Coming back from a demotion or termination is difficult and certainly worthy of advice, but in this chapter we address another employment dilemma that offers challenges: promotion to an executive position. Promotions are typically preceded by high-quality work performance—an employee does a good job at a previous position and, as a result, is promoted to a higher position. But all promotions are not success stories, especially those at the executive level. It is important to understand the layers of the executive transition and why executives fail in the transition period.

Definition

The executive transition is the period during which new leaders transition into an executive-level position and work their way to competence and productivity. In this period, new executives transition—physically and mentally—from their previous positions to leadership positions in which they must build credibility and competence. The emotional aspects of the transition involve leaving one organization behind, gaining acceptance at another, and putting leadership skills on display to see whether an approach will be accepted or rejected. The transition period is the most significant period of any new executive's career, but it is often undervalued, partly because it varies according to the individual and the situation. Michael Watkins (2003), author of *The First 90 Days*, described transitions as both "periods of opportunity, a chance to start afresh and to make needed changes in an organization" and "periods of acute vulnerability, because [new leaders] lack established working relationships and detailed understanding of [their] new role" (p. 1). What new leaders do or do not do in this window tends to be carved into their brand for a long time. New leaders who appropriately match their leadership and management style and adjust to the campus climate increase their likelihood of long-term success, while those who fail to accurately read the dynamics of the new situation—mismatch leadership approach with current reality—face a difficult transition, if not eventual termination.

Length

We define the transition period from the moment an executive agrees to accept the position through the break-even point, "the point at which new leaders have contributed as much value to their new organizations as they have consumed from it. . . . New leaders are net consumers of value early on; as they learn and begin to take action, they begin to create value" (Watkins, 2003, p. 2). How long does this take? Is it the first 90 days, the first 100 days, the first year, or the first 3 years? Publicly traded companies measure the transition period on the basis of results new executives produce in the first 90 days—the period associated with stock performance. Franklin D. Roosevelt established the 100-day transition period for U.S. presidents when he took office in 1933 in the midst of the Great Depression—he had to move fast to pull the nation toward recovery and, thus, declared the first 100 days as a benchmark for future presidents. In practice, the length of the executive transition period depends on individual traits (experience, education, skills, emotional intelligence, adaptability) and organizational characteristics (size, complexity, politics, culture, and personnel). The many possible combinations of these factors make it almost impossible to suggest a general length of the transition period. That said, a key marker of the closing of the transition period is the point at which new leaders begin consistently making positive contributions to the organization—according to Watkins (2003) this is the break-even point.

Challenges and Opportunities

For new executives, the transition period is full of challenges and opportunities. Challenges are often difficult for newcomers to decipher because most challenges are embedded in the culture of the environment; new executives encounter unwritten rules that do not apply evenly to everyone and are likely to introduce ambitious changes before they garner the necessary social capital to do so. Receiving critical feedback, which is essential for improvement, is difficult for executives because others tend to withhold bad news from them. This is especially problematic for new executives who need information to make leadership and management style adjustments. In the transition period, new executives may be asked to make critical decisions before they have adequate information, which puts them in a position to make mistakes or be viewed as indecisive. Priorities and performance expectations may be undefined, and the lack of clarity often leads to hesitancy and diminished confidence. Allies and enemies are difficult to distinguish, and subordinates have a distinct knowledge advantage over new executives. Yet the transition period is also full of opportunity. New executives can refine their image by eliminating previously unsuccessful management tactics and adopting more effective leadership strategies. They have a chance to score early victories by looking at old problems from new perspectives and devising seemingly novel solutions. Being new, they may be less restrained by some factors that hampered their predecessors, and they can establish new relationships and alliances. New executives bring different perspectives, fresh talents, and new intelligence to old problems; their contribution to the environment can be immediately positive because of their fresh perspective.

Costs of Failure

In his book *Topgrading: How Leading Companies Win by Hiring, Coaching, and Keeping the Best people,* Bradford Smart (1999) identified and estimated indirect and direct costs associated with executive transition failure. Direct costs for the organization include hiring (advertising, search firm fees, interview expenses, relocation packages, and signing bonuses); executive compensation for the duration of employment; maintenance (health insurance, travel, administrative support and overhead); and termination (severance, buyout agreements, legal fees, and exit packages). These expenses can amount to hundreds of thousands if not millions of dollars. Smart (1999) suggested direct costs to organizations can amount to 24 times the executive's base salary. However, direct costs pale in comparison to indirect costs—nonfinancial damages—to the organization. The most significant indirect cost is damage to the organization's reputation with investors, consumers, suppliers, and employees. Investors lose confidence in organizations that lack stability in executive positions; consumers and suppliers lose confidence when products and services are disrupted by turnover in senior leadership. Employee morale is adversely affected when workers must constantly readjust to a new leader and new organizational priorities.

Executives who fail to make the transition also face direct and indirect costs. Direct costs for them include relocation expenses, loss of retirement contributions, loss of income, and gaps in insurance coverage. These costs are multiplied if a family is involved. Although some direct costs may be reimbursed by the employer, most are not. Indirect damages are even more disruptive. Personal reputations and future employment opportunities are at risk when executives are terminated in the transition period. Future employers will inquire about a shortened tenure on a résumé. Rumors, true or untrue, about an executive's perceived failure can haunt him or her well into the future.

Failure Rates

Studies conducted by Morgan McCall and Michael Lombardo (1983) for the Center for Creative Leadership and Patricia Wheeler (2008) through the Alexcel Group and the Institute of Executive Development concluded that between 40% and 50% of new executives are pushed out, fail, or quit within 18 months. Executives fail in the transition period mostly because they cannot manage nontechnical challenges: leadership, communication, listening, and likeability. Wheeler (2008) surveyed 20,000 corporate executives in transition and discovered that 34% of transition failure was due to a lack of leadership and management skills; technical challenges—such as budget management and knowledge of operations—accounted for only 7% of transition failures. In most cases, these were highly competent executives who had held multiple positions leading to the executive role, so their experience and competence were not in question. On paper they had all the prerequisites to be successful at the next level, but they failed because of nontechnical competencies.

Reasons for Transition Failure

Why do almost 50% of competent, seasoned executives fail in the transition? Why would new executives who demonstrated mastery in previous positions, received rave reviews from previous supervisors and colleagues, and possessed the appropriate educational background struggle in the transition to new executive positions? Understanding transition failure is a prerequisite to navigating around such breakdowns. The literature offers a number of reasons why new executives fail.

Lack of Self-awareness

The Arbinger Institute (2010) blamed executive failure on a lack of self-awareness—blindness to how one's behavior affects others combined with an inflated sense of self-importance. Leaders who lack self-awareness have personality flaws that may not be obvious to themselves but are obvious to others; they are inconsiderate regarding how their behaviors create crisis for others and unaware of how their negotiation style stifles honest feedback. They are the last to know about their poor performance, because they are too proud to ask or because others deliberately withhold information from them. They see matters from their own perspective only and reject all evidence that might suggest otherwise. This personality flaw is masked by high levels of productivity in management positions, and once these people reach executive-level positions they produce only negative results. Lack of self-awareness is especially damaging in the transition, because it is the window of opportunity during which first impressions are made, important clues about the organization are on display, and new leaders need to listen most.

Feedback Voids

Daniel Goleman, Richard Boyatzis, and Annie McKee (2002), in *Primal Leadership: Learning to Lead with Emotional Intelligence,*

9

hypothesized that new executives fail when they create environments in which feedback voids exist. They called this "the CEO disease—the information vacuum around a leader created when people withhold important (and usually unpleasant) information" (p. 93). Timely feedback is critical to enable new executives to gauge whether their leadership/management approach is appropriate for the situation and is producing the desired results. Financial indicators tell one side of the story, but the other side is driven by feedback, and behaviors that stifle feedback are detrimental to the organization. New executives already face an uphill battle receiving feedback because the power difference between them and their subordinates creates unintentional barriers. Feedback voids are created when new leaders criticize truth tellers, dominate conversations, ignore advice, or punish messengers. Executives in transition are unlikely to receive the constructive criticism essential to improving performance if they are unable to create safe environments in which subordinates feel comfortable sharing the truth.

Absence of an Onboarding Plan

Executives often use the time between accepting a new job and the start date to relax. This can be a significant mistake. New leaders fail in the transition when they neglect to develop their own onboarding plan: a plan to identify what they need to know and prioritize what they need to do; a plan to assess inherent and personal risks; a plan to build a working relationship with the boss and negotiate parameters of success; and a plan to clarify the most important priorities of the position. New leaders stumble through the first year only to discover that what they were prepared to do does not match what was expected of them. In *The New Leader's 100-Day Action Plan*, George Bradt, Jayme Check, and Jorge Pedraza (2009) observed that many new leaders show up on the first day without a plan; neither they nor their organizations have thought about an onboarding plan. Too many new leaders fail to use the transition period to develop a game plan; instead they just show up on the first day of work and hope for things to work out. Bradt et al. (2009) advised that new leaders should pause long enough to think through and put a plan in place to accelerate during the transition period.

Misdiagnosis of the Situation

A key mistake in any leadership transition is not taking the time to diagnose the current situation and, instead, imposing a leadership approach that is not an appropriate fit. Watkins (2003) explained that the root cause of transition failure is new executives misunderstanding the demands of the new situation, combined with their inability to adjust their leadership style accordingly. He defined the ultimate challenge of the transition period as "a pernicious interaction between the situation, with its opportunities and pitfalls, and the individual, with his or her strengths and vulnerabilities" (p. 4). Therefore, a prerequisite for transition success is accurately diagnosing the situation and clarifying the leadership style requirements. Watkins described four types of situations new executives might encounter: (1) start-up, (2) turnaround, (3) realignment, or (4) sustaining success. In a start-up, new executives are responsible for assembling talent and resources to get the new operation up and running; in a turnaround, they are responsible for taking a unit that is in trouble and getting it back on track; in a realignment, the challenge is revitalizing a unit that is drifting off track; and sustaining success involves maintaining the productivity of a successful unit and advancing it to the next level. Different management and leadership tactics are required in each situation. Generally, time is critical in start-ups and turnarounds; leaders must rapidly diagnose the situation, move fast and aggressively, and take chances. The focus is on understanding problems and responding quickly. There is less urgency in realignments and sustaining success. These environments require understanding the culture and politics, using shared diagnoses to increase awareness among others of the need for change, and influencing opinion leaders. In these situations, it is more important to understand the organization, get the strategy right, and make good decisions early on. New leaders who inappropriately transplant their standard leadership style to a new situation risk being disconnected from their unit.

Overreliance on Past Success

When is too much success a bad thing? When that success affects your ability to view situations objectively and adjust to new circumstances. Marshall Goldsmith and Mark Reiter (2007) theorized that success in previous positions poises leaders for failure in new positions because "we get positive reinforcement from our past successes, and . . . we think our past success is predictive of great things in the future" (p. 16). In their book, *What Got You Here Won't Get You There*, the authors suggested that success leads new executives to cling to past management behaviors with the expectation that those behaviors will produce similar results in the future. Past success makes leaders overconfident of their ability to make things happen. They are filled with unflappable optimism and resist changes in their behavior. This seemingly logical notion—behaviors that produced success there should produce success here—can create negative results. Successful management behavior in one position does not always translate to the next position, because the combination of variables that make up the new environment and demands on leadership are likely to be different. Clinging to a "this is how we did it at my other job" mentality interferes with new learning and creates feedback voids. By the time a new executive discovers this flaw, it is often too late to reverse the damage.

Executive Transitions in Higher Education

Up to this point, our observations have been focused on the general literature surrounding executives in transition. We will now focus on higher education administration, specifically the role of the vice president for student affairs. Executive transition failure has not been as fully explored in academia as it has been in business, but the concepts—definitions, challenges, opportunities, costs, and reasons for failure—are parallel. With few exceptions, collegiate executives—presidents, provosts, vice presidents, and deans—and their institutions face the same transition challenges as their corporate counterparts. Both are subject to financial constraints, personnel and talent deficiencies, and pressure to improve operational efficiency. For both, failure in the transition period will likely come as a result of similar mishaps: lack of self-awareness, overreliance on past success, feedback voids, misdiagnosis of the current situation, and lack of an onboarding plan. Under normal circumstances, any one of these mishaps might not necessarily result in termination for a new educational executive, but mishaps in the transition period tend to be disproportionately damaging. Consider the case of John Mason.

John Mason, the vice president for student affairs at Great College, was aggressively recruited by East University for the same position. Mason had served Great College for 5 years, where he rebuilt a division of student affairs that was in shambles and had no strategic direction. His assignment at Great College was to "bring integrity back to the division and remove personnel who are holding back progress for their own interests." Taking charge in his first year, he terminated underperformers, implemented a new strategic plan, and eliminated duplicate programs. These actions resulted in a complete turnaround.

The president of East University was impressed by what he heard about Mason's work and wanted him to fill the vacant vice president for student affairs position. The search firm persuaded Mason to apply and interview. Mason became the successful candidate and was offered a salary 40% above his salary at Great College. He took the job at East University and immediately implemented the game plan he used to rebuild the Division of Student Affairs at Great College.

There was only one problem: The Division of Student Affairs at East University was not in crisis. The former vice president had moved on to accept a presidency, but he had left an excellent team. The division was performing at a high level and needed leadership that would sustain the current trajectory. Instead, drawing on his interpretation of why he was recruited and his past success, Mason selected a leadership path fit for a turnaround situation. He slashed programs, eliminated positions, and brought in his own leadership team. The team in place tried to explain to him that he was going down the wrong path, but he ignored their input because it was the same thing he heard when he was transforming the division at Great College.

After 12 months of turnaround leadership, Mason was called into the president's office. The president said, "I am sorry I was not clear with you about our expectations and did not have time to meet with you earlier. Your approach has alienated your staff and resulted in a number of legal challenges that we will be contending with for years. My only resort at this point is to offer you an opportunity to resign." Mason accepted a severance package and resigned immediately.

Mason made two classic transition mistakes: (1) He placed too much emphasis on his past management success, and (2) he failed to diagnose the current situation before choosing his leadership approach. He relied on what made him successful in his previous position and assumed that was why he was chosen for this position. He thought he was there to make the same kinds of changes he made at Great College. He did not take the time to understand and diagnose the situation and reset his game plan. Instead, he implemented the same formula he used at Great College. His reputation was so damaged by his approach during the transition that the president had no choice but to ask him to resign.

Transition Research Project

Mason's story is a reminder that nontechnical skills—namely, leadership and management skills—are essential in the transition period. Wheeler's (2008) survey of 20,000 executives is among the largest and most referenced surveys on executive transition failure. When executives were asked to rate reasons for transition failure, more than a third cited "lack of interpersonal and leadership skills" (34% percent). They failed because they could not build relationships, collaborate across units, and influence people. Surprisingly, "lack of technical skills/competencies" accounted for only 7% of executive failures. Typically, previous experience gives executives the requisite knowledge and technical skills to do a new job, but that experience does not necessarily prepare them for the complex task of executing those skills in a new environment and resetting their management approach. This task requires sophisticated nontechnical skills and attributes, such as personal discipline, empathy, interpersonal communication skills, likeability, and leadership abilities.

Inspired by Wheeler's (2008) research, Carry and Keppler (2013) conducted a survey to compare perceptions of transition challenges among aspiring and active vice presidents for student affairs. Active vice presidents were asked to rank their most significant technical and nontechnical challenges in the transition, while aspiring vice presidents were asked to respond on the basis of their perceptions of these challenges. The objective was to identify the gaps between actual and perceived transition challenges. The survey included these questions:

Question 1

To vice presidents: What were the most significant **technical challenges** during your transition period?

To aspiring vice presidents: What are the most significant **technical challenges** new vice presidents face during the transition period?

Budgetary constraints, personnel conflicts, crisis management, operational inefficiencies, strategic planning, understanding institutional governance, physical resources (equipment), physical resources (facilities), human resources, communication

Rank them from 1 to 10 (1 = most important, 10 = least important).

Question 2

To vice presidents and aspiring vice presidents: What do you think are the most significant **nontechnical challenges** responsible for stalling vice presidents during the transition period?

Lack of leadership and management skills, structural problems in the organization, goal conflicts with the organization, lack of support from the executive team, lack of personal skills/discipline, poor assignment with new role, unclear organizational priorities

Rank them from 1 to 7 (1 = most important, 7 = least important).

Methodology

Through an e-mail invitation, 35 active vice presidents for student affairs were invited to participate in a 15-minute phone conversation to complete the survey. Another eight active vice presidents completed the survey while attending a conference. Aspiring vice presidents were invited to complete the survey while attending the Institute for Aspiring Senior Student Affairs Officers sponsored by the National Association of Student Personnel Administrators. Respondents were asked to rank technical and nontechnical challenges from most to least significant; thus, the lower the average score, the more importance respondents gave to the specific challenge.

Participants

In total, 43 active vice presidents and 74 aspiring vice presidents completed the survey. Active vice presidents participated from all types of institutions: public, private, 2-year, and 4-year. Their college administration experience ranged from 5 years to as high as 49 years, with an approximate average of 28 years. Years as vice president for student affairs ranged from 5 to 36, with an approximate average of 9 years. The 74 aspiring vice presidents came from a wide variety of institutions and held positions in various student affairs areas (e.g., housing, assessment, judicial affairs).

16

More than 80% held titles of assistant or associate vice president or dean of students. Their college administration experience ranged from 5 to 36 years, with an average of 18 years.

Definition of Terms

Transition challenges were grouped into two categories: technical and nontechnical. Technical challenges were defined as those directly related to operational, financial, and personnel competencies of the position. Technical challenges are quantifiable, and proficiency requires a certain level of education, training, and experience. In this context, technical challenges include dealing with budget constraints, managing personnel conflicts, managing crises, dealing with operational inefficiencies, leading strategic planning efforts, understanding and navigating institutional governance, managing capital and human resources, and communicating clearly.

Nontechnical challenges are less quantifiable and not position-specific. To overcome these kinds of challenges, executives must draw on innate emotional intelligence rather than book smarts. The skills necessary to respond to nontechnical challenges are often teachable but are harder to quantify and observe. In this context, nontechnical challenges included structural problems in the institution/division, goal conflicts with supervisors, lack of support from the executive team, poor organizational fit, and unclear institutional/divisional priorities. These challenges require leadership and management skills and emotional intelligence to overcome.

The terms "active" and "aspiring" are used to describe, respectively, survey respondents who are currently serving as vice presidents for student affairs and those who self-identified as aspiring to become vice presidents (e.g., directors, associate and assistant vice presidents).

Results

Comparisons of responses from aspiring and active vice presidents are captured in Figures 1.1 and 1.2 and Tables 1.1 and 1.2. In each case, respondents were asked to rank the challenges in order of importance. The graphs include three data points: mean score on each challenge for aspiring, mean score on each challenge for active, and difference between the two scores. The tables show how the responses compare when placed in order from most important (lowest score) to least important (highest score).

In response to question 1, active and aspiring vice presidents both ranked budgetary constraints as the most important technical challenge. Average scores for active and aspiring vice presidents were 2.92 and 2.60, respectively. The difference between the two responses was 0.32, the smallest difference between any of the 10 compared responses. Both also ranked physical resources (equipment) as the least important transition challenge, with scores of 7.89 (active) and 7.31 (aspiring). Average scores and differences are illustrated in Figure 1.1.

Aspiring and active vice presidents showed the largest difference in their responses to human resources (difference = 2.60) and personnel conflicts (difference = 1.92). Aspiring vice presidents ranked human resources (6.05) and personnel conflicts (5.33) as significantly less important than active vice presidents did (3.45 and 3.41, respectively). This difference is most apparent when the comparisons are placed in rank order (see Table 1.1). Aspiring vice presidents ranked budget (2.92), institutional governance (4.73), and strategic planning (4.81) as the top three transition challenges. Active vice presidents ranked budget (2.60), personnel conflicts (3.41), and human resources (3.45) as the top three. This difference in ranking offers a key insight into how active and aspiring vice presidents view the priorities of the role, and the distinction carries over into how new vice presidents approach the position.

Figure 1.1

Comparison of Responses to Most Significant Technical Transition Challenges

(Aspiring Vice Presidents versus Active Vice Presidents)

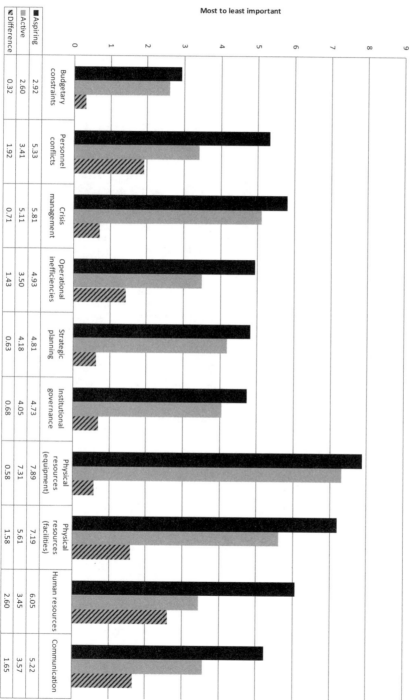

		Aspiring	Active	Difference
	Budgetary constraints	2.92	2.60	0.32
	Personnel conflicts	5.33	3.41	1.92
	Crisis management	5.81	5.11	0.71
	Operational inefficiencies	4.93	3.50	1.43
	Strategic planning	4.81	4.18	0.63
	Institutional governance	4.73	4.05	0.68
	Physical resources (equipment)	7.89	7.31	0.58
	Physical resources (facilities)	7.19	5.61	1.58
	Human resources	6.05	3.45	2.60
	Communication	5.22	3.57	1.65

Most to least important

Table 1.1

Comparison of Responses to Most Significant Technical Transition Challenges (Aspiring Vice Presidents versus Active Vice Presidents)

Aspiring Vice Presidents N = 74		Active Vice Presidents N = 43	
Budget	2.92	Budget	2.60
Institutional governance	4.73	Personnel conflicts	3.41
Strategic planning	4.81	Human resources	3.45
Operational inefficiencies	4.93	Operational inefficiencies	3.50
Communication	5.22	Communication	3.57
Personnel conflicts	5.33	Institutional governance	4.05
Crisis management	5.81	Strategic planning	4.18
Human resources	6.05	Crisis management	5.11
Physical resources (facilities)	7.19	Physical resources (facilities)	5.61
Physical resources (equipment)	7.89	Physical resources (equipment)	7.31

In response to question 2, the active and aspiring vice presidents were more closely aligned. Differences on all seven challenges were less than 2 (see Figure 1.2). Both groups agreed that unclear organizational priorities and structural problems are the two most important nontechnical challenges in the transition period. They also agreed that poor role assignment and lack of personal skills were the least important nontechnical challenges. Although the difference between mean scores for lack of personal skills was the highest (1.89), this category still ranked among the lowest transition challenges.

Figure 1.2

Comparison of Responses to Most Significant Nontechnical Transition Challenges (Aspiring Vice Presidents versus Active Vice Presidents)

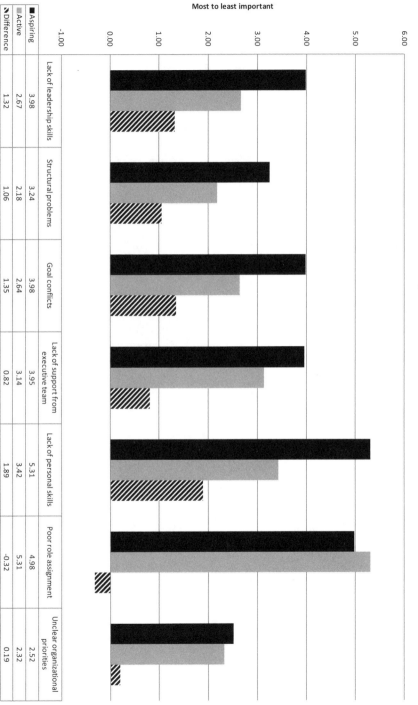

	Lack of leadership skills	Structural problems	Goal conflicts	Lack of support from executive team	Lack of personal skills	Poor role assignment	Unclear organizational priorities
■Aspiring	3.98	3.24	3.98	3.95	5.31	4.98	2.52
▨Active	2.67	2.18	2.64	3.14	3.42	5.31	2.32
▧Difference	1.32	1.06	1.35	0.82	1.89	-0.32	0.19

Most to least important

In Table 1.2, nontechnical challenges are arranged in order from most important to least important on the basis of responses. The table shows a high degree of consistency, with the exception of goal conflicts, which is ranked fifth by aspiring vice presidents and third by active vice presidents.

Table 1.2

Comparison of Responses to Most Significant Nontechnical Transition Challenges (Aspiring Vice Presidents versus Active Vice Presidents)

Aspiring Vice Presidents N = 74		Active Vice Presidents N = 43	
Unclear organizational priorities	2.52	Structural problems	2.18
Structural problems	3.24	Unclear organizational priorities	2.32
Lack of support from executive team	3.95	Goal conflicts	2.64
Lack of leadership skills	3.98	Lack of leadership skills	2.67
Goal conflicts	3.98	Lack of support from executive team	3.14
Poor role assignment	4.98	Lack of personal skills	3.42
Lack of personal skills	5.31	Poor role assignment	5.31

Discussion

Problems for vice presidents in transition exist in the gap where perception and reality differences are the greatest—where challenges of the current reality are vastly different from perceived challenges. In this gap new vice presidents spend lots of time resolving crises, putting out temporary fires rather than addressing strategic priorities. Even the most intentional and strategic planners will be confronted in the transition by seemingly urgent crises that tend to divert their attention away from important decisions. It is common for new vice presidents to thoughtfully identify priorities (e.g., financial management, personnel conflicts, strategic planning) to concentrate on during the first 90–100 days. However, it is highly likely their plans will be sidetracked by emergencies like a hazing allegation, a sexual assault case, a student death, or an employee termination. This makes it exceedingly important that new vice presidents have an accurate picture of the current reality rather than preconceived notions of the situation. Therefore, the real challenge in the transition is to quickly identify what is most important and put it on a track toward resolution; the urgent must be handled, but not at the expense of the important.

Four important conclusions emerged from the comparison of priorities among active and aspiring vice presidents.

- Confronting personnel and human resources challenges. Active vice presidents reported that personnel conflicts and human resources are the most pressing challenges in the transition. They reported spending a disproportionate amount of time sorting through unresolved personnel and human resources issues, including salary inequities and unqualified staff holding key positions. Working with the human resources department to resolve issues such as these can be surprisingly time consuming, especially when the vice president is new to the institution and is trying to learn a new set of rules. Most active vice presidents admitted delaying these kinds of decisions in the transition period, trying to gather additional information, or hoping that the matter would resolve itself, which frequently only exacerbated the problem. Most vice presidents who did not resolve personnel issues during the transition later wished they had. Establishing a strategic plan and understanding the demands of institutional governance are important, but when personnel and human resources matters exist, they should be resolved sooner rather than later. The longer they linger, the more likely they are to grow out of control.

- Understanding that 'it depends.' A number of active and aspiring vice presidents initially responded to Carry and Keppler's (2013) survey questions about ranking transition challenges by saying, "It depends." Transition challenges depend on the situation, timing, and institutional climate. It is difficult to rank the challenges without more information about the particular situation. This is why it is important to treat each transition experience individually and evaluate the current reality. Efforts to copy and paste a set of circumstances or employ the same leadership style in a new environment will likely produce poor results. Careful analysis of the current situation is essential to determine the optimal leadership style and to prioritize tasks. It is a mistake to assume that all executive transitions are governed by the same challenges and, thus, apply the same leadership behaviors; this is how even the best leaders lose credibility.

- Recognizing the reality of budget constraints. Although transition challenges vary depending on the situation, both aspiring and active vice presidents agreed that budgetary challenges are the top concern (see Table 1.1). Financial resources have always been a constraint for student affairs programs and services; vice presidents face even more significant financial challenges today, as institutions seek to protect their core business—academic degree programs—from budget cuts. Vice presidents of nonacademic programs and services have to make tough decisions about which programs, services, and personnel will stay and which must be eliminated. This challenge is magnified for new vice presidents who have to make difficult financial and personnel decisions during their transition periods. Starting a new job with a mandate to cut your budget by 5%, 10%, or 20% is a hard way to begin. Most new vice presidents do not know enough about the division they are inheriting or the institution to make smart budget decisions, and they often do not have enough social capital to avoid criticism. However, failing to act on financial decisions in the transition period can send the wrong message about the new executive's competence.

- Gaining clarity about the current reality. Transitioning into an institution that has unclear, undetermined, or frequently changing priorities is a significant undertaking. Unclear organizational priorities (lack of defined goals and objectives to guide decision making and accountability) were ranked among the most significant transition challenges by aspiring and active vice presidents. A lack of clear priorities leads to the unraveling of strategic initiatives, wasted time, and hesitation. New vice presidents for student affairs must spend a significant amount of time in the transition period gaining clarity on the current reality and organizational priorities. Even to the point of periodically checking in with the president to make sure they are on the right track and taking care of what he or she thinks is important. Equally important is making sure those under the supervision of the vice president are clear about the priorities. People make mistakes and become anxious when they are not sure what is important; priorities help guide how work is done and where resources are spent.

Chapter Summary

The transition is an extremely critical period for new executives in both education and business, and the circumstances and challenges that lead to failure or success are similar in the two fields. In the transition period, new executives solidify their brand, connect with the institution, and learn how to navigate in the new environment. If they do not achieve these benchmarks, they will fail. Transitions are filled with challenges and opportunities; overcoming the challenges and capitalizing on the opportunities is the foundation for success.

🛈 Making the case for transition education. Executive failure comes at a high cost—direct and indirect—to both the institution and the new vice president. Executives are highly susceptible to failure if they lack self-awareness, create feedback voids, do not have an onboarding strategy, misdiagnose the current situation, or rely heavily on past management success. For these reasons, executive onboarding is critically important. Institutions and new vice presidents must share responsibility for making executive transition planning a top priority and a condition of employment. Institutions must invest in customized onboarding development programs for executive-level positions—programs that unveil the most important nuances of the organization and prepare new vice presidents for success. At the same time, new vice presidents must take responsibility for developing and executing their own onboarding strategies.

- A physical, mental and emotional transition. The executive transition period involves a physical, mental, and emotional transition from one role to another. In the transition period new vice presidents must leave one institution, rethink their leadership approach, and find acceptance in a totally new environment. The transition period is complicated and more important to long-term success than one might imagine.

- How long is the transition period? A big mistake made by new vice presidents is underestimating the length of the transition period. Is it the first 90 days, the first 100 days, or the first year? The length of the transition period is impossible to predict because it is dependent upon the many combinations of individual traits and organizational characteristics. The best way to think about the length of the transition period is that it begins when the new vice president accepts the position and ends at the break-even point—the point at which a new vice president contributes more value than he or she consumes.

- The cost of failure is high for everyone. Executive failure bares an enormous cost for both new leaders and institutions. Losing a new vice president during the transition period includes direct financial costs and indirect emotional costs. Damage to the institution's reputation, diminished employee confidence, and slowed momentum will be far more detrimental than financial costs. The institution and the new executive must be fully invested in a successful transition period.

🔟 Confronting personnel and human resources challenges. In Carry and Keppler's (2013) study, active vice presidents reported that personnel conflicts and human resources are more pressing challenges in the transition. They reported spending a disproportionate amount of time sorting through unresolved personnel and human resources issues, including salary inequities and unqualified staff holding key positions. Working with the human resources department to resolve issues such as these can be surprisingly time-consuming, especially when the vice president is new to the institution and is trying to learn a new set of rules. Most active vice presidents admitted delaying these kinds of decisions in the transition period, trying to gather additional information or hoping that the matter would resolve itself, which frequently only exacerbated the problem. Most vice presidents who did not resolve personnel issues during the transition later wished they had; one said, "In hindsight, I wish I had taken care of those personnel issues sooner. Today it's tougher for me to deal with because of more urgent challenges." Establishing a strategic plan and understanding the demands of institutional governance are important, but when personnel and human resources matters exist, they should be resolved sooner rather than later. The longer they linger, the more likely they are to grow out of control.

References

Arbinger Institute. (2010). *Leadership and self-deception: Getting out of the box* (2nd ed.). San Francisco, CA: Berrett-Koehler.

Bradt, G., Check, J. A., & Pedraza, J. E. (2009). *The new leader's 100-day action plan: How to take charge, build your team, and get immediate results.* Hoboken, NJ: John Wiley & Sons.

Carry, A., & Keppler, K. (2013). [Comparisons of priorities among aspiring and active vice presidents for student affairs]. Unpublished raw data.

Goldsmith, M., & Reiter, M. (2007). *What got you here won't get you there: How successful people become even more successful.* New York, NY: Hyperion Books.

Goleman, D., Boyatzis, R. E., & McKee, A. (2002). *Primal leadership: Learning to lead with emotional intelligence.* Boston, MA: Harvard Business Review Press.

McCall, M. W., Jr., & Lombardo, M. M. (1983). *Off the track: Why and how successful executives get derailed* (Technical Report No. 21). Center for Creative Leadership, Greensboro, NC.

Smart, B. (1999). *Topgrading: How leading companies win by hiring, coaching, and keeping the best people.* Upper Saddle River, NJ: Prentice Hall.

Watkins, M. (2003). *The first 90 days: Critical success strategies for new leaders at all levels.* Boston, MA: Harvard Business Review Press.

Wheeler, P. (2008). *Executive transitions market study: Summary report 2008.* Atlanta, GA: Alexcel Group and Institute of Executive Development.

CHAPTER 2

Onboard Yourself

Ainsley Carry

*At most institutions, new employees begin their tenure by partici-
pating in a formal orientation process coordinated by the human
resources department, at which they receive basic information essential to starting work. Although this information is important,
it is woefully insufficient for preparing incoming educational executives to face the complexity of leading in the new environment.
Most new executives make avoidable, sometimes terminal, mistakes during the transition period. The only onboarding they can
count on is what they provide themselves. The author extrapolates
from his own experience to offer an empowering approach for new
vice presidents to bring themselves up to speed. The goal is to equip
new vice presidents with enough knowledge to feel confident, avoid
mistakes, and make informed decisions.*

While serving as an associate vice president, I was invited by a
recruiting firm to apply for a vice presidency. After discussing the
opportunity with my family, the search consultant, and my supervisor, I
applied for the position. With the help of friends and colleagues, I prepared
for a series of interviews, including phone, airport, and on-campus. I leaned
heavily on the wisdom and advice of colleagues and the search consultant
to help me think through my preparation. Out of the pool of candidates,

about a dozen were invited to airport interviews, and three were eventually invited to participate in on-campus interviews. In the end, I was selected as the final candidate. In 3 months I wrapped up my old job, moved my family, took some vacation time, and started work as a new vice president for student affairs.

I had no idea what was ahead of me. Although I sought advice from experienced vice presidents for student affairs, I was unprepared for the complex challenges ahead: trust gaps between senior administration and staff, territorialism, employees in the wrong jobs, and primitive policies and procedures. These issues were compounded by an institutional culture that was resistant to change and steeped in tradition. Before my first day on the job, I did not learn enough about the executive management culture, the politics of decision making, and unwritten rules. Later I learned that the position itself was steeped in controversy, there had been an internal candidate who desperately wanted the job, the incumbent had no budget or office space, and the responsibilities were grossly exaggerated on the organization chart to attract high-caliber candidates. I made many assumptions on the basis of what I assumed were standard features of a vice presidency, did not ask the right questions of the right people, and failed to see some red flags. I wanted the job. I was in competitive mode with a laser focus on winning the position and did not step back far enough to question irregularities. In hindsight, I realized that my first year could have been more effective if I had known how to onboard myself.

Institutions of higher education often do a poor job of onboarding new executive-level administrators. In general, they do little to make expectations and related challenges clear; they do not share the unwritten rules and politics of decision making; they do not identify potential landmines; and they do not deal with complicated personnel matters before new executives come on board. These jobs are complex and filled with potential pitfalls. Executives who are terminated or resign in the first 2 years are usually the victims of a lack of transparency or an expectation gap.

Onboarding—the practice of bringing new executives up to speed on organizational issues, priorities, and operations before their first day on the job—is a corporate business practice that has not been generally adopted in higher education administration. Much like for-profit companies, colleges and universities are distinct cultures with complex systems. Onboarding in these environments is especially important for executives in transition. For-profit corporations understand the importance of adequately preparing new executives, but institutions of higher education tend to neglect this important practice. Only in rare cases do academic institutions offer an onboarding process for new executive-level administrators.

Vice presidents for student affairs cannot afford to wait while institutions figure this out. Onboarding holds the key to long-term success. It helps the new executive avoid critical mistakes and clarifies important relationships. The transition period is too important for new vice presidents to assume that someone will provide an onboarding plan; they must take responsibility for their own onboarding experience. In this chapter, I explain onboarding, suggest a few reasons why universities do not onboard, and offer guidelines to help new vice presidents for student affairs onboard themselves.

Executive Onboarding

Executive onboarding refers to a comprehensive approach used by an employer to bring a new executive into the organization and up to competency as soon as possible. This is not the same as new employee orientation. The objectives of executive onboarding are to accelerate new executives' rate of knowledge acquisition and increase their capacity to make informed decisions; the sooner newcomers are prepared to make decisions, the sooner a corporation can continue to grow and see profits. Through structured interactions, new executives are thoroughly informed about resources, personnel issues, politics, pending legal matters, cultural nuances, and hidden agendas. Onboarding is not a substitute for traditional new employee orientation; rather, it is customized to the executive and the organization, focused on strategic issues, and deeply revealing. Onboarding delves into the institutional and interpersonal dynamics essential for new executives' success.

Onboarding is most often described in textbooks as an employer responsibility. Theoretically, employers are responsible for gathering pertinent briefing materials, arranging meetings with senior administrators, and surrounding new executives with the people they need to help them transition. For example, an employer that takes responsibility for onboarding might arrange a series of information sessions on key operating areas and issues, designate a representative from human resources to describe personnel issues, or assign a senior-level colleague from outside the formal reporting relationship to serve as a mentor to interpret organizational practices. Employer-directed onboarding involves introducing new executives to relationships that will enable them to build the social and political capital required for success.

When new executives are properly onboarded, all parties—new executive, organization, direct reports—benefit. For new executives, onboarding accelerates and clears their path to competence, shows them how to avoid career-ending mistakes, helps direct their energy to the highest priorities, teaches them how to get things done in the new environment, and helps them develop a deeper understanding of the organization. Onboarded executives begin work confident, competent, and ready to move forward. Organizations benefit from onboarding new executives, because prepared newcomers are more likely to be retained through the difficult transition period and can avoid the productivity lag that typically follows an executive hire. Direct reports benefit when new executives enter the organization/division with an understanding of the current reality—operational, technical, and political—and priorities.

However, onboarding does not guarantee success nor is it a prescriptive guide. New executives might learn about the organization's culture, politics, critical issues, and dynamics, but how they use that information is still their responsibility. Onboarding focuses on increasing competence, but new executives are ultimately responsible for how they use the information to fashion their own leadership and management behaviors. It is not an antidote for an inadequate leader or a bad hiring decision. Even with a comprehensive system, new executives are still susceptible to fit and skill mismatches. There is no step-by-step guide to onboarding for all situations; every process is unique because every situation—new executive and institution—is unique. Employer-directed onboarding procedures should be customized to the needs of the new executive and the current reality of the organization. Onboarding, no matter how thorough, will not compensate for executives who are not ready.

Why Universities Do Not Onboard

Onboarding new executives is common practice among the best corporations in the world. Target, The Home Depot, American Airlines, Toyota, and many other companies have devised sophisticated systems to prepare executives for the rigors of their new jobs. High levels of executive retention and productivity at corporations that employ these practices justify their use. Corporate human resources professional associations estimate that almost 50% of new executives fail in the first 18 months—the majority because of mismatches between their leadership approach and the reality of the situation (McCall & Lombardo, 1983; Smart, 1999; Wheeler, 2008). Universities face similar challenges in transitioning new executives such as presidents, vice presidents, and deans. Why aren't universities more intentional about onboarding these executives?

Aside from the formal new employee orientation orchestrated by human resources departments, most universities do not offer executives the kind of in-depth briefing that is essential for success in the transition period. Consider the following scenario:

> *Helen Martin was selected through a national search process as the new vice president for student affairs at North College. Mike Powell, an internal candidate for the position, was a 20-year employee and a senior member of the division. He was disappointed that he was not selected as the successor to his mentor and vowed to undermine his new boss.*

Martin hit the ground running in her first year by focusing on building an ambitious strategic plan. She consulted with faculty, staff, and her leadership team to create a plan for the division. In her previous role as an assistant vice president, she had coordinated strategic planning efforts and focused on tasks that needed to be done. In her first year at North College, she launched a number of initiatives. To her surprise, many of the initiatives were met with resistance by students and staff.

Powell did not warn Martin that student and staff governance groups were an important part of the university's decision-making culture, and ideas that did not emerge from them typically were met with resistance. He did not support many of the new initiatives and, behind her back, let others know of his displeasure with her leadership.

At the end of Martin's first year, it was obvious that many of her initiatives lacked buy-in and were not a priority of the larger organization. As a result, she had to start over. She spent her second year rebuilding relationships and her reputation. Her credibility as vice president was severely damaged.

What went wrong? Martin did not have the benefit of an appropriate onboarding. She underestimated Powell's influence and power to undermine her plans and did not calculate how his lack of commitment to her success would subvert her goals. She was never informed that student and staff governance groups were such an important part of the decision-making infrastructure and that they could stall good ideas if they were not consulted. She overrelied on previous management experiences and approached strategic planning as she did in her former role as an assistant vice president; in that role she could afford to be more of a taskmaster, because the vice president was responsible for maintaining relationships. In her new role as vice president, she needed to spend more time focused on maintaining relationships in the strategic planning process and leave the task driving to others. Her approach was also self-centered; she tended to push others along rather than share a compelling vision that inspired others to follow. And she assumed that the division needed a change agent when in fact the situation called for a different leadership style. All this information would have been communicated in a proper onboarding process. Onboarding would have helped Martin make better decisions about her approach and priorities during the transition period.

This scenario is not uncommon in higher education; in fact, it probably occurs more often than not. The scenario has all the ingredients of a disaster in the making: a new vice president hired from outside, a disgruntled subordinate who is less than cooperative, and leadership that follows a path that is contrary to the culture. Maybe someone will point out the new executive's errors; however, the truth is usually kept from the new leader until it is too late to undo the damage to his or her reputation. This type of damage leaves a scar on the executive's brand that is difficult to repair.

At least three barriers limit the adoption of executive onboarding in college administration: (1) University hiring practices for executives focus almost exclusively on technical competence and assume that new executives know what is needed to be successful (sink or swim flaw); (2) responsibility for onboarding new executives defaults to the human resources department and therefore assumes a compliance-focused agenda (human resources perspective); and (3) insiders are blind to the learning curve faced by newcomers (insider blinders).

Sink or Swim Flaw

In higher education, the attitude toward senior administrators in transition is sink or swim—either they have what it takes to figure things out or they do not. New vice presidents are left to fend for themselves in the transition, because the hiring process is largely based on measurable, observable technical competencies (such as educational background and career experiences) rather than less measurable character attributes (such as personality, temperament, leadership qualities, and likability). Search committees prefer to evaluate what candidates know through educational attainment, what they have accomplished through career experience, and what they can do through documented skills. Using these criteria, successful candidates are those who convince selection committees that they are the most competent person for the job, not necessarily the best fit in terms of temperament and leadership skills. The search process is designed to identify the most competent candidate; it assumes that the chosen candidate already knows what to do and how to do it: "We hired a smart vice president; she should know what is expected and figure out how to get it done." Although new senior administrators may be quick to identify what is expected, they may not know how to get it done in the new environment. Because of this overreliance on competence in the hiring process, new executives are left to figure out the nuances—sacred cows, politics, personnel issues, cultural norms, informal power structures, and interdepartmental conflicts—on their own.

However, blame for the sink or swim mentality does not rest totally with the hiring institution; in some cases, new vice presidents are the architects of their own shortcomings. Those who enter new environments overconfident about their knowledge, skills, and abilities tend to shun onboarding assistance. Vice presidents who are stepping into a second vice presidency or taking a vice presidency at a smaller institution can be overconfident and chill attempts by others to offer advice. Seasoned vice presidents think they know enough to bypass help and instead rely on past knowledge. This is a mistake, because no two institutions are exactly alike in their situation and leadership demands. Every new vice president for student affairs must take the time to learn the new environment and must never assume that his or her past experience is an indicator of future performance. Overconfidence in one's abilities can contribute to the sink or swim flaw.

Human Resources Perspective

Institutions of higher education fail to adequately onboard new senior administrators because this responsibility typically defaults to human resources departments. Almost every institution offers a form of orientation designed to provide new employees with necessary paperwork and a broad overview of the institution. New employees learn about institutional history, organizational structure, work roles, and the social environment. Generic activities are delivered through print materials, lectures, videos, and computer-based presentations. Basically, the orientation process is intended to offer new employees sufficient information to start work and receive a paycheck. As it is currently designed and delivered, the process does nothing to prepare senior administrators for the complex challenges they will face. From a human resources perspective, executive onboarding is defined by additional forms, procedures, and compliance issues. These departments are not equipped to provide the depth and breadth needed for customized onboarding. The human resources perspective is focused on policy compliance. The process is designed for the masses and not customized for new senior administrators. Thus, a new vice president will likely go through the same orientation experience as any other new staff member.

To further illustrate the point that human resources departments tend to view onboarding through the lens of compliance, consider two position announcements for onboarding coordinators, one from a public institution and the other from a private institution. These announcements were posted in nationally circulated publications. Names of institutions have been removed. The first position announcement is from the public institution.

Responsibilities: Generates banner IDs and cross-matches to avoid duplication; populates appropriate banner screens to trigger e-mail address, username, and onboarding process; processes confirmation of job offers that reflect position title, salary, exempt status, and start date contingent upon funding and all hiring documentation and employment requirements being completed; tracks formal acceptance of job offers; communicates and ensures completion of new hire checklist, which outlines employment requirements such as degree/licensure/certification verification, criminal background check, employee health clearance, I-9 forms, etc., and onboarding requirements such as tax forms, direct deposit, parking, benefit enrollment, and university, technology, manager, and care orientation dates/times; processes confirmation receipts to new hires upon satisfactory completion of all onboarding documentation; notifies appropriate university parties that new hire checklist is complete; assists in tracking annual foreign tax exempt status and visa expiration; maintains records of all job offers and employment and onboarding documentation, which includes scanning and indexing all new hire documentation and attaching appropriate documents to online requisition (PeopleAdmin system); closes requisitions for staff positions; and notifies applicants that position has been filled.

Although the term *onboarding* is used throughout the position announcement, the focus is on administrative tasks associated with new employee orientation. The position announcement describes compliance activities rather than true onboarding. The following is a position announcement for an onboarding coordinator at a private institution:

Position summary: Reports to the manager of staffing, administers the university's background screening program for staff hired through human resources and academic professionals hired through the dean of faculty. During the implementation period of approximately 18–24 months, the coordinator will create the framework for the program, to include developing university policies and procedures to support enhanced background screening. Serves as a principal source of information for candidates and hiring managers regarding background screening policies and procedures. This position also partners with the Office of

Environmental Health and Safety to oversee the post-offer pre-employment physical examination screening program. Reviews the outcome of the assessments and communicates adverse hiring decisions to candidates and hiring managers. Manages the onboarding process for staff hired through human resources. This includes assisting new hires with the relocation process, coordinating the new hire orientation program, ensuring that new hire information/paperwork is processed, and performing related onboarding activities.

Neither position announcement will produce a candidate who can customize trainings for new vice presidents for student affairs. Unless human resources departments are specifically instructed to do otherwise, the onboarding processes they develop will resemble an extension of existing new employee orientation. New senior administrators need in-depth knowledge of their operations to make appropriate management decisions during the transition period.

Insider Blinders

Another reason institutions of higher education do not typically onboard new executives is that insiders are not attuned to the obstacles faced by newcomers entering the culture. Insiders do not realize how much the translucent culture influences behavior and guides decision making. Every institution has its own culture and ways of getting things done, and people inside the culture cannot fully articulate it or understand how it hinders newcomers. Insiders are oblivious to the challenges faced by newcomers and therefore do not think onboarding is necessary. Meanwhile, newcomers stumble over institutional terminology, hidden/informal governance structures, unwritten procedures, unpublished exemptions to policy, and unclear expectations—nuances that have become standard operating procedures. The culture has become so well established that insiders do not understand why newcomers might think these practices are odd or hard to learn. Those working inside a system grow immune to the complexity of the culture, politics, and idiosyncrasies.

A second problem generated by insider blinders is that insiders are ill-equipped to orchestrate a comprehensive onboarding plan. They are so embedded in the culture that they cannot see the subtleties of the environment that influence success. For example, they might not think to explain why a particular board member has power over a broad range of decision making or why the chief financial officer has more influence than the president. When asked to explain these nuances, insiders typically reply, "That's just how it has always been done." They do not realize that these subtleties are crucially important for new administrators to understand.

Executive onboarding is overlooked in higher education because of a sink or swim mentality that overrelies on competence, a human resources perspective that focuses on compliance, and insider blinders that cannot see the barriers for newcomers. New vice presidents should not wait for their employers to take responsibility for their onboarding. They should reasonably expect their new employer to provide them with a proper orientation to begin work, but they must take onboarding—acceleration of knowledge about the new environment—into their own hands.

Onboard Yourself

With a high possibility that new senior administrators in higher education will not benefit from an employer-directed onboarding plan, new vice presidents for student affairs are advised to orchestrate their own plans. Strategies for executive transitioning are readily available in books such as *The First 90 Days* by Michael Watkins (2003); *Right from the Start* by Dan Ciampa and Michael Watkins (1999); *The New Leader's 100-Day Action Plan* by George Bradt, Jayme Check, and Jorge Pedraza (2009); *What Got You Here Won't Get You There* by Marshall Goldsmith and Mark Reiter (2007); *Good to Great* by Jim Collins (2001); and others that focus on preparing new executives. Although the advice offered in these texts is written with corporate executives in mind, the strategies are applicable to executives in almost any field.

In *The One Thing You Need to Know,* Marcus Buckingham (2005) theorized that peak performance in managing, leading, and sustaining individual success depends on one simple concept: clarity of message. He suggested that the antidote to anxiety is clarity. People make mistakes and become anxious when they are not sure what is important. Buckingham noted, "Confusion retards everything, from efficiency and focus to teamwork and partnership all the way to pride and satisfaction" (p. 76). Use the tools described below to gain clarity, and focus on sharing information with others.

The objective of onboarding is to make the first day on the new job feel like the end of the first year. To achieve this goal, new vice presidents need to onboard themselves by consuming information at a superhuman rate. To prepare for this undertaking, before the first day of work a new vice president should conduct a document analysis (history); collect staff profiles; conduct a SWOT analysis; and interview key stakeholders (current reality and priorities). *when & how soon?*

Conduct a Document Analysis

Read everything before the first day on the job. Information about the institution, division, campus culture, and challenges is available in annual reports, student and local newspapers, the school yearbook, board meeting minutes, and strategic plans. Consider reading documents dating back at least 3 years. Look for major themes and priorities: culture, challenges, strategies, finances, and ambition. For example, strategic plans and annual reports that propose standard operating procedures disguised as goals suggest a need to focus on the basics and get in line with that focus. A longitudinal look at the same sources will reveal major themes about landmark moments and major accomplishments; these documents offer insight into student concerns and possible lingering issues. Public universities are required to make their board meeting minutes available to the public. Minutes of board meetings reveal the types of decisions the board is involved with and a history of student affairs issues addressed at this level. Information extracted from these resources offers new vice presidents a foundation for strategic planning and prioritizing. Studying these documents offers a glimpse into what has been tried in the past and what opportunities have the best chance of success in the future.

Collect Staff Profiles

Before arriving on campus, learn as much as possible about the staff and talents in the division. Effective leaders and managers spend a lot of time evaluating talent and providing feedback. A staff profile is a collection of biographical information on staff members in key positions, from program coordinators to assistant vice presidents. The depth of this list may vary depending on the size of the division—smaller divisions (100 or fewer employees) may allow for staff profiles to be collected on all positions. The staff profile offers an overview of staffing talent—knowledge and experiences—and it is an efficient tool to memorize employee names and backgrounds.

A key question will be "How should I collect this information?" Consider the following suggestions, but the best approach depends on the context and institution. Staff profile information can be collected via résumés or on an electronic spreadsheet. Ask staff members in key positions to submit a current résumé to your administrative assistant; the administrative assistant can mail the résumés to you. Request employee information such as name, position title, years of experience, years at current institution, degrees earned and institutions, and experience at previous institutions.

Conduct a SWOT Analysis

A strengths, weaknesses, opportunities, and threats (SWOT) analysis is a review of internal and external threats to the organization. The SWOT analysis should be completed at the divisional and departmental levels. What are the risks for the division and for each department? A SWOT analysis is a good tool for learning about both long-term and short-term threats. Some issues will need to be addressed immediately (e.g., student safety, financial irregularities), while others will be less urgent and can be addressed as part of a long-term strategic plan (e.g., academic partnerships, housing expansion projects). Patterns and themes—financial issues, staff development, customer service, and salary equity—will emerge from the SWOT analysis as departments respond. The most critical tasks for an incoming vice president are prioritizing issues that emerge in the SWOT analysis and addressing the most important ones in a timely fashion; new vice presidents who are slow to identify or act on crucial deficiencies will be labeled ineffective. Methods used to collect this information will differ by institution; you might assemble an internal transition team made up of leaders in the division or work through a chief of staff or executive assistant.

The SWOT analysis is primarily an effort to assess risk factors. Bradt et al. (2009) provided a list of potential landmines and risks that have derailed new executives. Every executive position is laced with organizational, positional (role), and personal risks. *Organizational risks* are inherent to the organization and exist naturally; they are common in environments where the mission and strategy are unclear. In these environments, criteria for performance and measures of success are unknown; therefore, newcomers might be blamed for mishaps. *Positional risks* primarily arise out of the history of the position and the alignment of expectations with resources; expectations are unlikely to be met if resources are not properly aligned to accomplish stated goals and objectives. *Personal risks* are gaps in the new vice president's strengths, motivation, and fit for the position. New vice presidents face personal risks when the written and unwritten requirements of the position do not match their skill set or when personal and institutional values are misaligned. The key is to identify these risks as soon as possible, determine whether they are manageable, and find ways to mitigate or disarm them.

Interview Key Stakeholders

Every scrap of information about the division is important to the incoming vice president for student affairs. Document analyses, staff profiles, and SWOT analyses are valuable tools to begin the information-gathering process. But one of the most effective techniques for gathering pertinent information is face-to-face conversations: interviewing. Interview key stakeholders to unearth valuable information about the division. Interviewing offers the added benefit of building a relationship: People appreciate being asked their opinion and spending time talking about things that matter to them.

Several categories of people can offer valuable information to a new vice president for student affairs: colleagues, campus partners, your predecessor, your supervisor, student leaders, and board members. Colleagues (other vice presidents) can offer perspectives on the executive management culture, supervisor expectations, and existing challenges that could otherwise take years to uncover. Campus partners (e.g., academic deans) relish the opportunity to share ideas with an incoming senior administrator because of the possibility of establishing or strengthening the partnership. Predecessors, if they are willing to share, have valuable insight about sacred cows and landmines; they can share critical information about challenges faced during their tenure. However, some predecessors are not willing to share advice with newcomers, or their advice is tainted with bitterness. Be careful not to adopt burdens handed down by predecessors. Student leaders offer an important perspective: New senior student affairs administrators must put their finger on the pulse of students and identify with their challenges as soon as possible. This responsibility cannot be handled through a proxy (e.g., the dean of students or an assistant vice president). Connecting with students in the transition period is crucial. Board members can offer insights about expectations for the role of the incoming vice president. They care about the institution, offer a unique perspective as accomplished graduates, and can be important allies in advancing student issues. (In some cases, you might need permission from the president to interview board members.)

Interviewing the president is a special situation. In the vice president's transition, no relationship is more important than the one with the president. Relationships with colleagues, other vice presidents, direct reports, campus partners, and students are important, but they all pale in comparison with the relationship with the president. The president holds the key to transition success, sets priorities, interprets the vice president's actions to stakeholders, validates progress toward priorities, and endorses access to resources. The president has more influence on a vice president's acceleration through the transition and long-term success than any other individual or group. Discussing key transition issues with the president to establish crystal-clear priorities is among the most important responsibilities for a vice president who is attempting to onboard him- or herself. In initial meetings with the president, try to arrive at agreement about the current reality, related challenges, and performance expectations. Proactively engage the president about his or her perspective. Vice presidents must determine whether the president's analysis of the situation is different from their own and close that gap as soon as possible. If the vice president and president do not see the current reality in the same way, expectations about results will come into conflict.

Interviewing is essential to help new vice presidents understand the current reality of the division they are inheriting. Watkins (2003) described the root causes of transition failure as "a pernicious interaction between the situation, with its opportunities and pitfalls, and the individual, with his or her strengths and vulnerabilities" (p. 4). He listed four types of organizational situations new leaders might find: (1) start-up, (2) turnaround, (3) realignment, and (4) sustaining success. Each situation calls for a different leadership approach. In start-ups (building from scratch or rebuilding), new executives must focus on assembling talent and resources. In turnarounds (taking a division in trouble and getting it back on track) new executives must quickly identify problems and implement solutions. Time is critical in start-ups and turnarounds. The leader must make a rapid diagnosis of the situation, take chances, and move fast and aggressively to meet the core mission; as a result, more energy is devoted to doing than to reflecting. In realignments, the challenge is to revitalize a division that has drifted off track. Sustaining success involves maintaining productivity of a successful division and advancing it to the next level. In realignments and sustaining success situations, timing is less urgent; persuasion and shared diagnosis are more effective to increase awareness and influence opinions. In these situations it is important for new vice presidents to understand the division, get the strategy right, and make good decisions. Success or failure of their leadership/management approach depends on how well it aligns with the current reality, not the reality of their previous institutions.

Once on Board

Onboarding is a superhuman effort to get up to competency and build confidence before the first day on the job. After the first day, the onboarding period does not end, but the activities change. Before the first day, the focus is on building knowledge; starting on the first day, the focus is on getting everyone on the same page. Two strategies can be effective in accomplishing this task: (1) host an onboarding retreat and (2) devise a comprehensive communication plan.

It is typical for executives in transition to take time off—to celebrate, move the family, squeeze in a vacation—before starting a new vice presidency. Taking time off is a perfectly logical thing to do considering the pending work demands, the stress of change, and the impact on the family. Most people would advise the new vice president to take a few weeks off before starting a demanding new vice presidency. I suggest just the opposite. The interim period before starting a new vice presidency is a critical time to accelerate learning. This is not the time to celebrate or take off; it's a time to get busy flattening the learning curve. It is a crucial window of opportunity to build common understanding on the current situation, negotiate joint expectations, build relationships, and start discussions on strategies for moving forward. New vice presidents should hustle to be competent enough to hit the ground running on Day 1 and not assume that they know what to expect. They should start preparing for the new environment as soon as possible. The first year is usually filled with unpredictable on-the-job demands; thus, the opportunity to set aside uninterrupted time to study the division is fleeting. Use this window of time to get on the same page with everyone else.

Host an Onboarding Retreat

One way to quickly connect with others is to host a multiday onboarding retreat/discussion. Within 2 or 3 weeks of starting the new position, assemble an executive team for a 2-day retreat. If the division does not have a formal executive team, invite assistant vice presidents, the financial or budget manager, the dean of students, and program directors. Ask them to clear their calendars for two consecutive days (it's not impossible—they do it to attend professional conferences). Invite them to an open and honest onboarding discussion. The purpose is to bring you up to speed on key pieces of information. The agenda should include in-depth introductions; a financial summary of the division, including pending capital projects; a discussion of the key themes from the SWOT analysis; a summary and discussion of major issues; a report of progress on the strategic plan; a review of campuswide issues (e.g., student complaints, departmental conflicts, debt, student discipline issues, history of the organizational structure); and crisis response responsibilities for the division (e.g., student death, sexual assault, missing student, protest protocol). Request the assembly of pertinent materials ahead of the retreat. Read all of it and compare it with what you have collected during the interview process and since. During the retreat, your role will be to seek clarity on key issues and facilitate joint understanding of priorities. In this kind of retreat, listening and learning are the key outcomes.

Devise a Communication Plan

In all leadership transitions there is a thirst for information; people want to know what is going on and how their roles might change. Take control by devising a communication plan. During the transition, people will make judgments about the new vice president. Every form of communication—verbal, nonverbal, written, spoken, action, or inaction—is a message and has the potential to shape what people think about you. Where vice presidents spend their time, the questions they ask, the people they eat with, and the battles they win or lose all send messages. Waiting too long to develop a communication strategy will allow rumors and nonverbal communications to become the perception and, by default, the truth. Once an inaccurate perception has been formed, it is almost impossible to correct. Be intentional about every communication in the transition period; realize that everything communicates something and not always what was intended. Think through details in communication right down to tone, timing, and room setup.

In Chapter 5, Gage Paine offers a personal look at communication as a tool for vice presidents in transition. Through the story of her own vice presidential transition, she emphasizes the importance of sharing what you care about, using presence and listening, employing social media, and asking good questions as communication strategies. Communication is one of the most neglected aspects of executive transitions, but it is the most important element of a new vice president's success.

Chapter Summary

In the best case scenario, new vice presidents for student affairs should be welcomed with an employer-directed onboarding plan that prepares them to competently face challenges through the transition period and beyond. In the worst-case scenario, new vice presidents have to figure things out on their own and devise their own onboarding strategy. Onboarding yourself is an empowering approach for new vice presidents to take responsibility for bringing themselves up to speed on what they need to know and do to be successful in the new job. The intention is to equip them with enough knowledge to feel confident, avoid mistakes, and make informed decisions.

⊕ Institutions of higher education usually do not offer comprehensive onboarding plans for new executives because: (1) they overly on competence in the hiring process and assume that new executives know what to do to be successful (sink or swim); (2) responsibilities for executive onboarding default to human resources departments and take on a compliance-focused agenda (human resources perspective); and (3) insiders are blind to the magnitude of the learning curve for new executives (insider blinders).

🛈 New vice presidents should take full responsibility for onboarding themselves. Waiting for the employer to provide information is not a wise strategy. In most cases, institutions of higher education will not think to provide the in-depth onboarding education executives need for success. Taking responsibility reduces the chances that you will not have important information.

🛈 Before the first day of work, new vice presidents need to gather and consume information at a superhuman pace. Their goal is to feel confident and prepared to make sound decisions. To reach this point, they should *conduct a document analysis* of key documents of the division and institution, to establish an understanding of historical decisions and issues; *collect staff profiles* to learn about members of the division and their talents; *conduct a SWOT analysis* to identify internal and external threats to the division; and *interview key stakeholders* (student leaders, board members, colleagues, campus partners, and the president) to triangulate important themes and build relationships.

🛈 After the first day on the job, new vice presidents should turn their focus to getting everybody on the same page. After building their own competence and confidence, the next task is reducing gaps between what they understand and what others understand. To accomplish this they should *host an onboarding retreat/discussion* to share information and jointly determine priorities for moving forward and *devise a communication plan.*

References

Bradt, G., Check, J. A., & Pedraza, J. E. (2009). *The new leader's 100-day action plan: How to take charge, build your team, and get immediate results.* Hoboken, NJ: John Wiley & Sons.

Buckingham, M. (2005). *The one thing you need to know: . . . About great managing, great leading, and sustained individual success.* New York, NY: Free Press.

Collins, J. (2001). *Good to great: Why some companies make the leap . . . and others don't.* New York, NY: HarperCollins Publishing.

Ciampa, D., & Watkins, M. (1999). *Right from the start.* Boston, MA: Harvard Business Press.

Goldsmith, M., & Reiter, M. (2007). *What got you here won't get you there: How successful people become even more successful.* New York, NY: Hyperion Books.

McCall, M. W., Jr., & Lombardo, M. M. (1983). *Off the track: Why and how successful executives get derailed* (Technical Report No. 21). Center for Creative Leadership, Greensboro, NC.

Smart, B. (1999). *Topgrading: How leading companies win by hiring, coaching, and keeping the best people.* Upper Saddle River, NJ: Prentice Hall.

Watkins, M. (2003). *The first 90 days: Critical success strategies for new leaders at all levels.* Boston, MA: Harvard Business Review Press.

Wheeler, P. (2008). Executive transitions market study: Summary report 2008. Atlanta, GA: Alexcel Group and Institute of Executive Development.

CHAPTER 3

Cultural Challenges
Keys to Thriving in the Transition

Brian O. Hemphill, Melanie V. Tucker, John R. Jones III, and Susan M. Gardner

Transitioning into a vice presidency brings myriad challenges, including quickly adapting to the campus culture. Viewing the vice presidency and the organization through a cultural lens provides a frame of reference, yet it can be difficult to identify the subtle nuances that can cause new vice presidents to make early mistakes. The critical first steps for the newly appointed vice president for student affairs can determine whether he or she will be embraced by the campus community or viewed as an outsider. This chapter addresses four strategic activities: researching the institution, identifying the unwritten rules for executives, embracing the culture, and strategically implementing change. All four have a tremendous impact on the success or failure of new vice presidents.

For new vice presidents for student affairs, the transition period brings challenges of learning and adapting to the culture of a new university community. In higher education, culture is the mutually shaped pattern of institutional history, mission, physical settings, norms, traditions, values, practices, beliefs, and assumptions that guide behavior of individuals and groups (Kuh & Whitt, 1988). Although culture in part creates a sense of community and inspires loyalty, every institution's culture is different (Birnbaum, 1988; Kuh & Whitt, 1988). Viewing institutional life through a cultural lens provides a frame of reference with which to interpret the meaning of events and actions (Kuh & Whitt, 1988). Not understanding the culture of the university is the most frequent cause of significant mistakes for new vice presidents. Of crucial importance, especially before implementing any changes, is the newcomer's grasp of established culture.

The first steps a new vice president for student affairs takes can determine whether he or she will be embraced by the campus community or viewed as an outsider. If the latter is the case, the vice president will have a short tenure. Four strategic activities will have a tremendous impact on the success or failure of vice presidents as they transition into a new university community. These activities are: (1) researching the institution, (2) identifying the unwritten rules for executives, (3) embracing the campus culture, and (4) strategically implementing change. In addition to these activities, new vice presidents need to factor in their own cultural expectations and how those expectations align (or do not) with the campus culture. Vice presidential candidates can begin working on these activities before they receive a job offer and should continue to work on them indefinitely.

This chapter includes personal stories from the four authors. These accounts are shared anonymously to provide details without worry of perceived criticism toward institutions or individuals. These stories represent real experiences with resulting hard-earned insight.

Doing the Research

It is vital that a candidate for vice president for student affairs researches and assesses the campus culture before accepting a position. Research, in this context, means trying to understand the unique aspects of the campus environment and gaining an appreciation for aspects of the university that inform and impact daily functioning. Just as the institution conducts a search process to find a candidate who is a good fit, the candidate should examine how his or her own philosophy, beliefs, and values fit with the culture of the institution. This examination will help the candidate determine whether the position is a good professional and personal fit. An in-depth look at the culture of the institution, campus do's and don'ts, norms of the community, and the institution's vision and mission will enable a comparison with one's professional philosophies and core values.

One way to assess whether prospective vice presidents fit the campus culture is to use a three-pronged approach that includes: (1) evaluating the organizational, professional, and geographical culture (Watkins, 2003); (2) determining whether the culture aligns with professional values and personal needs; and (3) identifying whether the candidate can flourish in the new environment. Candidates should start by analyzing the culture of the campus and the surrounding community. Organizationally, candidates will benefit from identifying such things as how decisions are made, receptiveness to change, and how quickly or slowly change has occurred in the past. Professionally, candidates may benefit from identifying such things as support for travel; time for writing, teaching, or external leadership roles; and expectations for involvement in social activities outside the 8 to 5 time frame. Geographically, candidates should evaluate whether the surrounding community aligns with their own values. For example, candidates may wish to know whether the region is progressive or conservative, religious or secular, diverse or homogenous, and so on. There is no right or wrong answer in this process; the goal is to determine whether the new vice president will fit in, both professionally and personally.

Prospective vice presidents should search online materials or ask the person who will be the immediate supervisor to answer these questions:

1. What do you view as the student affairs role in bringing your strategic vision to life?
2. What do you consider to be the most important aspects of this job?

3. What are the primary challenges that must be addressed within the first 6 months?

Personal fit in this context is tied to professional and personal growth. Are you looking to be a change agent or to uphold the status quo? Are you seeking an opportunity to affect the direction of the institution or support the direction that is already in place? Be cognizant of biases that faculty and staff may hold regarding institutional expectations, administrative demands, and the influence of the environment on and off campus. Determine which aspects of the culture you are willing to accept and which would be difficult to accept. Of the latter, which might you as vice president be able to alter? This level of examination can help you avoid missteps in navigating institutional politics early on. No institution is perfect; thorough research enables prospective vice presidents to make informed decisions about professional and personal fit.

In addition to assessing cultural fit, you should understand the power structure within the organization, the institutional priorities, the untouchable traditions and beliefs, how decisions are made, and how the institution responds to changes and difficulties. This examination will help you anticipate potential conflicts over priorities and astutely navigate those conflicts. New vice presidents must apply due diligence before and during the transition to ensure individual fit and to establish a solid foundation for continued career success.

Personal Perspective: The Role of Research

As I started to search for my first vice president's role, I searched broadly, both geographically and in type of institution, thinking the act of earning a vice president's position would be success in and of itself. However, I quickly learned that true success would be found in becoming a vice president in a place where my core values were aligned with the mission and vision of the institution. During my first on-campus interview for a vice president position, I quickly realized that the campus culture was not one in which I could flourish. The vice president was expected to terminate several employees and dismantle a handful of departments during the first 6 months, with no foreseeable options to rebuild, rehire, or renew. Though I could not have identified the depth of these expectations before the interview, I realized that I had skimped on the research process on the front end, thinking I would have time on the back end to find the information I needed to make informed decisions.

To determine alignment and avoid applying to institutions that were not going to be a good fit, I needed to do research throughout the application process. After I withdrew my candidacy for that position, I committed myself to factoring in time for research before applying for a position, to more productively narrow my search. I was able to search not only on the basis of geography, which was an essential factor for me, but also on institutional aspects such as diversity of student body; commitment to access and inclusion; the mission and vision embraced by the institution and division; the depth and breadth of strategic planning; and institutional buy-in to the value of student affairs. Through my research, I identified a handful of vice president positions I thought would be a good fit for me. I hoped I would be a good fit for one of them.

By narrowing my search according to my core values and aligning those with values embraced by the institution, I avoided having to withdraw my candidacy or decline further interviews, neither of which feels good nor contributes to a positive professional reputation. When I was researching the institution where I ultimately started my first vice presidency, before setting foot on campus, I requested information from the search chair when I could not find what I was looking for online; read broadly (from the student newspaper to institutional financial reports); talked to colleagues who knew the executive administrators at the institution; and investigated community aspects such as housing costs, economic growth, and social opportunities. Quality of life outside work is as important to me as quality of life at work.

The research I did before, during, and after the interview process enabled me to identify deal makers and deal breakers if I was offered the position. I was able to confidently negotiate my contract, both financially and with regard to the intangible aspects that would allow me to be successful. Without the research I had done throughout the process, I would have missed key opportunities during negotiations to line up

Identifying Unwritten Rules

As they gain an understanding of various institutional cultures, new vice presidents will find that college campuses are rich in institution-specific traditions, symbolism, beliefs, and ceremonies. In university settings, rituals such as orientation, academic convocation, student functions, ceremonial events, and annual gatherings are social constructs that communicate values, socialize new members, and celebrate accomplishments (Taylor & von Destinon, 2000). Many of these rituals, often viewed as untouchable traditions, serve as standards through which members of the culture assess, define, and refine their behavior (Kuh, 2000). They are nonnegotiable in terms of significant modification before a new vice president becomes indoctrinated into the culture. Understanding which traditions are untouchable is essential for success at the executive level.

An institution's culture has unspoken rules based on shared values and beliefs that inform how work is done and what is rewarded. New vice presidents should tread cautiously with colleagues in the president's cabinet, at least until a familiarity has developed. Unfortunately, many vice presidents learn about unwritten rules by innocently breaking them through ignorance of the culture and expectations. These mistakes can have grave consequences for new vice presidents as they strive to build credibility and respect.

Asking questions and observing other executives is the most direct way to learn the unwritten rules. However, a more prudent way to gain an understanding of the rules is by developing a strong relationship with the new boss: the president. Allow time to secure and strengthen this relationship. A new vice president should identify and recognize the biases, strengths, and weaknesses of the president in order to skillfully represent the interests of the division (Moore, 2002). Knowing the president's expectations will translate into personal confidence when dealing with the political dimensions of the new environment (Moore, 2002). Developing and strengthening this relationship should begin before the official start of the job; vice presidents who wait until they arrive on campus impair their ability to secure early victories. Identifying and understanding the boss's expectations, both written and unwritten, provides a strong foundation to make informed decisions about short-term and long-term planning.

New vice presidents should also develop relationships with other executives—the provost, vice presidents, and academic deans—as they will provide a pathway for building coalitions, resolving conflicts, and creating consensus. These relationships will enhance understanding of campus culture, which will help advance the division (Moore, 2002). As with the president, understanding the unwritten expectations of other executives will inform and shape the new vice president's decision making and behavior. For example, the "meeting before the meeting" is a common practice; it is where delicate proposals gain or lose support before being formally presented to the president and cabinet. Determining whether this practice exists and how to engage it is essential to avoid early missteps.

As new vice presidents build relationships, they should keep in mind the lens through which each executive views his or her role in the institution. Collectively, these varied views of reality can help identify consistent themes and potential pitfalls. Do not take one person's opinion as fact for any particular unwritten rule; look for repeated themes, patterns, and confirmations. Avoid breaking the unwritten rules by answering the following questions:

1. How does communication really happen?
2. Who are the circles of influence?
3. Who drives decision making?
4. Who has influence with the president and the provost?

New vice presidents should spend time engaging faculty and informing them of issues and concerns involved in serving students. You can have a direct impact if you inform faculty opinion makers and leaders about student affairs issues (Miller, 2000). One unwritten rule is related to how much faculty input is factored into decision making. For example, in some shared governance environments, faculty leaders expect to be asked to informally sign off on student affairs decisions that might affect academic affairs. Thus, in addition to understanding what other executives consider unwritten rules, you should know what unwritten rules faculty leaders hold sacred. Understanding faculty perspectives that influence the campus culture can help you understand the broader cultural context and identify strategic opportunities.

New vice presidents who employ the following three strategies are likely to succeed in navigating the unwritten rules: (1) Observe everything—people who follow the unwritten rules are usually rewarded; (2) establish trusting relationships—find a mentor or colleague who can fill in the gaps and answer questions; and (3) use effective communication—actively communicate with those you seek to influence. Communication must be consistent, frequent, and of high quality, and must include listening and feedback (Moore, 2000). Most new vice presidents will eventually master the unwritten rules. If these rules are not aligned with their core values, they must decide how they will navigate conflicts in a socially and politically correct way while maintaining credibility (Bolman & Deal, 2008). However, if the unwritten rules and the new vice president's core values are aligned, it will lead to credible leadership, successful navigation of relationships, and mastery of political situations.

Practical Advice: The Danger of Unwritten Rules

In my first job as a vice president, I reported to someone I had worked with at a previous institution. I assumed that I was familiar with his preferences, leadership style, methods of communication, and expectations. Because I had developed a familiarity with this person in another role, I was not thorough in identifying unwritten rules. While I did some questioning of rules and expectations, it was a cursory and superficial effort. I made some initial decisions based on assumptions formed earlier in my career.

Because I made some erroneous assumptions about the unwritten rules, I was not prepared to articulate these rules to the people with whom I worked. My understanding of the rules changed when my assumptions were challenged; therefore, I sometimes appeared to be inconsistent with regard to my expectations of others. I learned that I needed to reaffirm, question, and validate unwritten rules in spite of my previous connection with the president, and I needed to share those rules with the people who worked for me.

Two months into my new vice presidency, the chair of the threat assessment team heard about a student of concern. On the basis of her experience with the team, the chair acted quickly to pull together information to formulate a plan, but she did not immediately inform me. In fact, I heard of the potential threat from another vice president. By the time I was up to speed with details about the threat assessment team's plan of action, the president and campus police had been pulled into the equation.

Because I was not the one who laid the groundwork for the president and the police about the course of action, the final decision was taken out of my hands. Eventually, the situation was resolved in an appropriate and acceptable manner, but the process was messy, stressful, and cumbersome. In processing with my team afterward, I realized that I had not done a good job of communicating with them the unwritten expectations to which I was being held.

Often we do not know what we need to know until we need to know it. This is especially true of unwritten rules. We cannot always predict what we will need to know to be successful. It comes down to asking questions, building relationships, and sharing information. Learning the unwritten rules is not a one-time thing; situations change over time and when a new president joins the institution. Vice presidents must consistently ensure that they and their teams are aware of the unwritten rules.

Embracing the Campus Culture

Upon entering a new campus culture, vice presidents might jump to conclusions about why things are performed a certain way, and they might make decisions on the basis of their previous institution's process for handling a specific situation. Past experiences can help with current challenges, but the process might not be the same in the new environment. Do not be the new vice president who says, "Well, at my last institution, this is how we did it." A new vice president must embrace the campus culture, not only accepting the way things are done but developing a proactive mind set wrapped around the new culture.

To embrace the culture of your new institution, identify a time frame to transition mentally from the old position to the new position (Watkins, 2003). Create distance from the old role, and embrace the new role and new institution. Visualize yourself in the new role, think about differences in the current position, imagine thinking and acting differently, and recognize how your job will strategically align student affairs with the larger institution. For example, are you expected to attend multiple athletic events? Are you expected to attend few or many development/fundraiser events? Are you expected to delegate a lot or a little? What about crisis management?

Conversely, what are your own expectations? Do they include performing as the past vice president did, or will you be making changes? Develop a plan to transition cognitively, physically, and psychologically into the new role. Incorporate what you have already learned about the culture at the new institution. Be invested from the first day. Have a plan for success that fits the campus culture.

Vice presidents who do not take the time to understand and appreciate the culture of their new campuses are doomed to fail. They are expected to learn the culture and navigate within it to get things done. This does not mean they cannot be themselves; rather, it means they need to figure out how to be themselves in a new culture. New vice presidents are expected to figure out how to integrate their past experiences and lessons into an entirely new environment.

Developing a Transition Plan: Cultural Influences

When I started as a new vice president for student affairs, I thought a transition plan meant putting pen to paper and creating a complex outline about what I wanted to accomplish in 3 months, 6 months, a year, and so on. I was mistaking a work plan for a transition plan. A work plan should come, in part, from the direction received from the new supervisor. But a new supervisor is not always able to tell an incoming vice president how to navigate the politics and culture of the institution; that is where a transition plan is important. A transition plan is not a list of things to accomplish; rather, it is a plan for successfully transitioning into the executive role on multiple levels, including embracing the campus culture, building relationships, and concretely establishing oneself as a vice president.

To develop my transition plan, I attended two student orientations, a campus forum, and a faculty in-service before my start date. Before appearing on too many people's radars, I was able to observe who some of the movers and shakers were on campus and mentally note a few things I wanted to change or address later in my tenure. This background informed how I embraced becoming a vice president and helped me prioritize my work plan.

To transition into the vice presidency with a clean slate, I intentionally left some materials from my previous position at home in the attic. This forced me not to lean on old resources and ideas. The visual presence of these materials at home in storage and their absence from my office reminded me that I could not remain in my old mindset. I could not rely on what had worked at other institutions.

Another aspect of my transition plan included moving slowly as far as laying claim to territory and rearranging "closets"— issues, programs, and services that need to be observed, assessed, and possibly revamped or rearranged. When I started as a new professional years ago, I rearranged a closet outside my office within a week of my arrival. The experience that ensued was something I hope never to repeat. Since then, when I start a new position, I always look for closets I should not rearrange (at least not right away). Space can be a huge campus issue, and who owns it can be a reflection of relative power. My transition plan included not assuming that I had control of all space in the student affairs area. This awareness played out in my work plan as well, as I built in time to pay attention to the figurative closets in my division.

One aspect I did not include in my transition plan, which I wish I had, was being careful about whom to trust. Within weeks of starting the job, I made friends with an academic dean. In what I believed was a confidential conversation, I shared some of my concerns about campus programs and policies. Weeks later, I discovered that the dean had passed this information along to another vice president, who in turn shared it with the president. Needless to say, my next conversation with the president was not a pleasant one. I learned that it is important to spend time observing campus interactions—learning the dynamics and inner workings of relationships—before choosing friends and allies who will provide reciprocal support.

Another component I wish I had incorporated into my transition plan was allowing myself time and patience. By nature, I am not a patient person. I often joke that I need to stop praying for patience and start praying that I am blessed with fewer situations that require it. The person I was least patient with as a new vice president was myself. I wanted to absorb everything like a sponge within a few weeks and feel confident and secure in my new role. It may sound like a cliché, but it is normal to feel like a fish out of water for a year or longer as a new vice president. It takes time to adapt to a new culture and to understand campus policies, procedures, and politics. Build that time into your transition plan. Understand that others on campus are trying to figure out how you work as well. Be patient with those who have questions, even when they are questioning a decision you made. Learn to listen more than speak in these situations.

Incorporate Change, But Move Cautiously

The fourth strategy is to promote change judiciously. Often, new vice presidents for student affairs are hired as change agents. In response to perceived or real shortcomings in the division, political dimensions of the institution, or people in the organization, vice presidents may make the mistake of believing they must produce immediate change. Many components of university life affect campus acceptance of change. New vice presidents should consider how best to implement change—not only on an organizational level, as vice president for student affairs, but from a personal perspective as well.

Making Organizational Changes

Organizational changes need to be accomplished over time. To envision and effect organizational change, new vice presidents must be familiar with institutional governance and the patterns of power, politics, decision making, communication, and conflict. This understanding can only occur over time; the vice president must allow realistic expectations to emerge and visualize the steps required within the existing culture.

Before you implement divisional changes, ask yourself the following questions:

1. Is there a mandate for change from the president?
2. What factors in the institutional culture, history, or external environment might affect the acceptance of change?
3. Is the campus ready to change? If not, what can be done to create a more receptive climate for change?
4. Is there a strategy to manage institutional response as the change process unfolds?

Prioritize changes, being thoughtful about multiple small changes and selective about large-scale changes that entail high risks as well as high rewards. When there is a mandate for change, some people will jump in without a plan. This can be disastrous if the change is not successful. Identify the time frame in which change is expected, and develop a plan to make the change within the known constraints. When there is not a mandate for change, be even more judicious—selectively implement changes to maximize reward and minimize risk.

Personal Attributes Influence the Acceptance of Change

With dialogue and observation, it may be easy to identify the factors that affect the acceptance of change at the organizational level, but the same cannot always be said for implementing change on a personal/individual level. These factors are more subjective in nature and are not as frequently discussed. For example, gender stereotypes and bias continue to exist with regard to leadership (Bolman & Deal, 2008), and they may influence how a new vice president is perceived and how well change is accepted. Research indicates that men continue to be perceived and preferred as leaders, and consistently evaluated more positively than women leaders (Gresham, 2009). New female vice presidents should be attuned to the presence of other women in executive leadership positions, as this can provide some insight into the acceptance (or not) of gender differences among executives (Pasque & Nicholson, 2011).

Leaders who make changes can be viewed as assertive and domineering, traits often positively associated with men but negatively associated with women (Eagly & Karau, 2002). Women executives who make changes too quickly are often unfairly penalized (Gresham, 2009), while women who wait too long to make changes are often viewed as less effective. Regardless of gender, an essential element for a new vice president is confidence in one's own identity before coming into the role. You can expect to encounter institutional and cultural pressures to conform and compromise in ways that can lessen your ability to be an agent of change.

Another example of how gender can affect the acceptance of change is through work/life balance. While both men and women may seek work/life balance, there remains a stereotype that women have more family obligations. Work/life balance is often considered a reflection of a new vice president's commitment to the institution. This is not to say that new vice presidents should not attend to family matters; rather, it is to acknowledge that these expectations will have an effect on the rate at which the culture buys into proposed changes. Work/life balance should be important to everyone, but new female vice presidents should be mindful that many executive administrators still have an old-fashioned view of women in leadership roles.

As they develop transition plans and identify changes to implement, new vice presidents with family obligations may want to consider flexibility to accommodate these obligations, time away from the office, and the availability of flextime. Be realistic about how long it will take to implement changes and the professional and personal energy each one will require.

Finally, new vice presidents should be cognizant of personal attributes that affect the acceptance of change. For example, be aware of leadership and management behaviors and how they affect others. Awareness of personal characteristics that can subtly or significantly help or hinder the acceptance of change will go a long way toward helping you find success.

Institutional Change: One Woman's Story

I became a vice president as a single mother under 40 years of age. I was young, and I looked even younger. In addition, I was still in the process of completing my dissertation. Not having a terminal degree left me with little clout among the faculty. Although I had more than 15 years of higher education experience, my perceived youth created a barrier to success. Early on, I heard many hallway conversations alluding to perceptions of my lack of experience based solely on how young I looked. This situation informed my perception of the campus culture and instilled in me a desire to demonstrate my ability to embrace and change the culture.

To demonstrate embracing the campus culture, I put finishing my dissertation on the fast track and worked countless evenings after my children were in bed to get it done. I believed that the degree would add credibility to my position and to the division, because the campus culture valued academic affairs and teaching highly. If I were to advance the Division of Student Affairs, I needed faculty to see me as an equal partner in the educational mission.

Coming into the position, I was concerned that others not see me as a young mother who could not handle the demands of the vice president's role. Fair or not, I knew that stereotypes about mothers—particularly single mothers—existed. It was important to have a backup plan for as many situations as I could imagine, and to minimize the possibility of contributing to stereotypes I did not want to reinforce. I created a "village" of support, and this approach informed how I moved forward in attempting to influence (and change) the campus culture.

Although my children are in school now, I still face the challenges of finding child care after school and transporting them to dance classes, music lessons, and basketball games. Fortunately, my children's grandparents are nearby and I am surrounded by great friends and now a supportive husband. This village is my Plan B when I get stuck in a board meeting that runs late or when a student is in crisis. I joke with my staff that I leave the office each night to go home and start my second shift. I have also been known to quip about being the mayor of the village that helps with my children. My experience with juggling the demands of motherhood certainly informs my work as vice president: I am able to demonstrate my ability to manage a number of priorities at the same time. I have gained the respect of faculty and staff and have become a sounding board for other mothers on campus. Motherhood also informs my work with students—both traditional and nontraditional—who are parents. I know the challenges they face on a day-to-day basis, and I bring compassion and empathy to conversations and interactions with them.

Even when holding others accountable, I find that compassion and listening are essential. In making changes in my division related to program development, staffing, and budget, I find myself using the village metaphor quite frequently. Before making budgetary decisions, for example, I assemble my student affairs team to discuss the benefits of the programs we offer. We center these conversations around assessment data, yes. But empathy and compassion allow me to effectively listen to my team and work directly with them before making budgetary decisions. I believe that this approach increases transparency in leadership. Even when others do not agree with my decision, they respect it because they know I worked directly with them to make it.

In embracing aspects of the campus culture (e.g., earning a doctorate to show my commitment to academic excellence) and challenging aspects of the campus culture (e.g., the mistaken idea that single mothers are unable to be effective vice presidents), I have influenced institutional culture by dispelling the myth that women can "do it all." No one—man or woman—can truly do it all. The word balance is thrown around a lot when people are talking about women in leadership positions. I do not like to think of my leadership this way. My work and my family are my priorities. It is just as important for me to walk down the hall in the morning and greet each member of my staff as it is for me to sit down and eat dinner with my children and my husband in the evening. I am often the first to tell my staff to go home at night. I have been known to forward the phones to my desk at 4:00 p.m. on a Friday and tell everyone else to go home. I encourage staff to take time to be with their parents and their children. I pay it forward. That is how I work toward improving and changing institutional culture.

Chapter Summary

New vice presidents for student affairs should never underestimate the power of institutional culture. They must find balance between maintaining key components of campus culture while seeking to advance the mission of student development. New vice presidents face a variety of leadership challenges and transition issues, but none is more complicated than adapting to the cultural nuances of a new university community. In this chapter, the authors discussed four strategic activities to effectively transition into a new culture. By undertaking these activities, new vice presidents can successfully build the relationships essential for success.

- Research the institution. Just as the institution conducts a search process to find a candidate who is a good fit, the candidate should examine how his or her own philosophy, beliefs, and values fit with the culture of the institution.

- Understand the unwritten rules. Institutions are rich in traditions, symbolism, beliefs, and ceremony. Unwritten rules are standards through which members of the institution assess, define, and judge behavior. The new vice president for student affairs must get a grasp on the unwritten rules early in the transition.

- Embrace institutional culture. Resist the urge to jump to conclusions about how things are done or how they should be done, especially if this perspective is rooted in your previous institutional experiences. First embrace the existing culture and seek to understand it.

- Move cautiously as a change agent. New vice presidents often think they were brought in to make immediate changes. Carefully evaluate this assumption before implementing an overly ambitious change agenda. Wrong assumptions and inappropriate actions could be a fatal combination.

As the personal stories illustrated, there is not one perfect way to transition into the role of vice president for student affairs. Undertaking the four activities discussed in this chapter may make for a smoother experience, but expect challenges along the way. The transition into becoming a vice president starts before you ever set foot on the new campus and continues well beyond the first year.

References

Birnbaum, R. (1988). *How colleges work: The cybernetics of academic organization and leadership.* San Francisco, CA: Jossey-Bass.

Bolman, L. G., & Deal, T. E. (2008). *Reframing organizations: Artistry, choice, and leadership.* San Francisco, CA: Jossey-Bass.

Eagly, A. H., & Karau, S. J. (2002). Role congruity theory of prejudice toward female leaders. *Psychology Review, 109*(3), 573–598.

Gresham, M. H. (2009, Summer). New wine in old bottles: Cutting a new path in the academy. *Forum on Public Policy Online,* 1–15. Retrieved from http://forumonpublicpolicy.com/summer09/archivesummer09/gresham.pdf

Kuh, G. D. (2000). Understanding campus environments. In M. J. Barr & M. Desler (Eds.), *The handbook of student affairs administration* (2nd ed.) (pp. 50–71). San Francisco, CA: Jossey-Bass.

Kuh, G. D., & Whitt, E. J. (1988). *The invisible tapestry: Culture in American colleges and universities* (AAHE-ERIC/Higher Education Research Report No. 1). Washington, DC: American Association for Higher Education.

Miller, T. E. (2000). Institutional governance and the role of student affairs. In M. J. Barr & M. Desler (Eds.), *The handbook of student affairs administration* (2nd ed.) (pp. 37–49). San Francisco, CA: Jossey-Bass.

Moore, P. L. (2000). The political dimensions of decision making. In M. J. Barr & M. Desler (Eds.), *The handbook of student affairs administration* (2nd ed.) (pp. 179–196). San Francisco, CA: Jossey-Bass.

Pasque, P. A., & Nicholson, S. E. (Eds.). (2011). *Empowering women in higher education and student affairs.* Sterling, VA: Stylus Publishing.

Taylor, S. L., & von Destinon, M. (2000). Selecting, training, supervising, and evaluating staff. In M. J. Barr & M. Desler (Eds.), *The handbook of student affairs administration* (2nd ed.) (pp. 155–177). San Francisco, CA: Jossey-Bass.

Watkins, M. (2003). *The first 90 days: Critical success strategies for new leaders at all levels.* Boston, MA: Harvard Business Review Press.

CHAPTER 4

Making the Internal Transition

Karen Warren Coleman

Transitioning into a vice president for student affairs position is an extraordinary and daunting experience. It is crucial to quickly assess the division's strengths and vulnerabilities, establish and then maintain trusted lines of communication with key stakeholders, and demonstrate deliberate and decisive leadership. Navigating this landscape as a vice president hired from within can be satisfying yet complicated. Vice presidents hired internally face greater expectations that they will lead with velocity because they understand the institution, know the key players, and can hit the ground running. In this chapter, the author discusses how the internal hire can capitalize on momentum while avoiding hasty decision making.

As vice president for student affairs, I often meet with young professionals who want to strategically plan a successful career path and advance in the profession. They assume that I followed a clear and logical path, that I knew exactly where I wanted to go, that my career opportunities presented themselves rationally, and that I followed an orderly decision-making process to get where I am today. Those in this profession know this is rarely the case. In reality, emerging professionals are best served by seeking out opportunities and jumping on them when they present themselves, even if that means diverging from the original plan.

This Was Always the Plan

When I graduated from the University of Massachusetts, Amherst, with a degree in psychology, I was torn between pursuing doctoral work in clinical psychology and applying to law school. The only thing I knew for certain was that I was not ready to make the decision. I loved my work in student affairs as an undergraduate and believed that the staff and faculty made an otherwise large and anonymous place feel incredibly accessible and intimate. I decided to work in the profession to see if it was a good fit and whether it would provide the clarity I needed. At the same time, I kept my options open by taking the LSAT. I knew my LSAT score would not expire for several years, so I could delay a decision about law school. Two years into my first professional position, I decided to pursue a master's degree in higher education administration at the University of Vermont. The idea of law school remained in the back of my mind for many more years.

While I have had opportunities and have made choices that have been intentional and often agonizing, I was less focused on a particular outcome or end during my early years in the profession. Over the years, supervisors and mentors have challenged me: "What are you trying to achieve?" "Where do you want to be in 5 years?" "What is your plan?" "What do you need to do to get there?" Eventually, I realized that I needed to become more deliberate about career choices. Now I regularly challenge my staff to think about the training and experiences they need to ensure that they are competitive for future professional opportunities.

A Big Opportunity

I had been associate vice president of student affairs and second in command for two and a half years when the vice president announced that she was stepping down. Only a few years earlier, I had arrived at the university, relocating from across the country and making the transition from associate dean of students with a small and fairly straightforward portfolio to associate vice president with a portfolio that was large, complicated, and unwieldy. My position was challenging and demanded a high degree of political acumen and managerial nuance. I was fortunate to have had great training at my previous institution—a large, highly selective public research university. In that job, getting things done required a lot of patience and strong partnerships across the campus. I supervised student conduct, assessment, human resources and budget, student legal services, and technology and marketing. It was a position that involved program and business expertise, a balance I enjoyed and one that I knew I would need if I were to advance in the profession.

I will never forget the summer I arrived on campus as an associate vice president. I had been on campus about 2 weeks and was scheduled to provide welcoming remarks at a late-summer training for residence hall housekeepers and engineers. The room was filled with at least 125 people gearing up for the new school year and catching each other up on family goings-on, children headed off to college, and new grandchildren on the way. I felt the buzz of excitement of a new school year, although it was muted by the thumping of my own heartbeat. These staff members, some of the longest serving at the university, were returning to a campus where many of their former colleagues had been laid off. What could I possibly say to this group that would not sound vacuous and trite? My position had just been created, and I was hired during an economic downturn. I was new, young, and paralyzed by self-doubt. But I had no choice; I had to step up and deliver my presentation. Afterward, some staff members told me how thoughtful my remarks were and that they communicated a sense of "leadership and authenticity." It was one of my first lessons on the importance of confidence and humility—exude confidence and practice humility. Whether I am presenting to a large audience or meeting with a student in my office, it is important I am authentic and that I connect with the listener(s).

Fast-forward 2 years and the vice president for student affairs was stepping down. Who was I to think I was prepared for this enormous role? The

73

nerve-wracking presentation to the housekeepers and engineers was now merely a blip in my memory; important and difficult at the time, but barely memorable in comparison with the things I had wrestled with as associate vice president in the 2 years since. While it was daunting to think about being responsible for 20 departments, a sizable annual operating budget, and a staff of roughly 350, I could not imagine not competing for it. It was an amazing student affairs opportunity at an important juncture for the university. I knew I could not live with the "not knowing" if I didn't try.

Some characteristics I love about my university are the same things that make me feel vulnerable. It is an environment of big ideas and persuasive arguments. Good ideas, tested through rigorous debate and dialogue, have the potential to become great ideas. At the same time, how this plays out among senior officers can be intimidating.

I Can Do This Job

Since my first speech on that hot summer day, I subsequently made countless presentations to hundreds of groups and achieved a level of confidence in my work competencies. I understood my portfolio, because I spent a great deal of time digging deeply into my areas. In my 2 years as associate vice president, I had led a universitywide global dining initiative in which the university selected new vendors and established a university department of dining services; created several new positions and eliminated others; and managed a number of complicated departmental audits. Through these experiences, I came to understand the university and how to get things accomplished, and I established strong and trusted relationships. Each of these experiences provided valuable insight into the division's strengths and deficiencies, what stakeholders understood about student affairs, and how I could realign units for greater effectiveness. I gained confidence in my grasp of the inner workings of the division and about the collaborative opportunities at the institutional level. I believed that not only could I handle the vice president job, I could do extraordinary things if given the opportunity.

I approached the task of making the decision to apply for the vice presidency as if I were writing an 800-page dissertation. In my brief tenure at the university, I had established myself as a committed leader who understood how to navigate a rigorous academic environment, but was I vice presidential material? I sought counsel from trusted colleagues and friends; their advice ranged from "You have to do this!" "You'll regret it if you don't apply." "You'll never know what could have happened!" to "You need to be really careful and be prepared for any outcome." "If you apply for the position and don't get it, you'll have to leave the university."

I had a good understanding of the university culture and an insider perspective on what was needed in the next vice president—the opportunities and challenges of the position. The university had ambitious plans for the next phase of campus and student life, so it was essential that the new vice president for student affairs be a strategic partner who would advocate for student needs, build community, and cultivate strong partnerships across campus and with board members. I also knew that the new vice president would have to quickly establish working relationships and communications with faculty, staff, students, alumni, friends, and the local community.

I was keenly aware that because I was associate vice president, I would be interviewing for the job through my work. Even though I had not submitted any formal materials, I was in a nonstop audition. From the moment the position became vacant to the moment I was offered the job, I was interviewing every day, in every conversation, in every meeting, for 8 months.

By the time I decided to apply, I had analyzed my decision from every conceivable angle, including what I would do if I did not get the job. I knew there were two possible outcomes to the scenario and I needed to be prepared for either. You do not know what things will be like until you are in a situation, but I knew I was not ready to leave the university, because my work had just begun, so I needed a plan. The interview process was a perfect opportunity to find out how my colleagues, university partners, trustees, and others felt about student affairs. How were we doing? What did we do well? What did we not do well? A search process can be a funny social experiment: People are often willing to be more critical and candid when they are explicitly given permission.

Being an Internal Candidate

I approached the multiphase interview process as an anthropological study: talking to trusted colleagues on and off campus about the opportunity; preparing the application materials; going through the on-campus interviews. I interviewed with almost 50 people over the expanse of the process. Throughout, I was laser-focused on making sure that, whatever the outcome, I would come out whole on the other side. During the interview process, I communicated with clarity about the mission of the organization, why I do this work, and why I was the candidate of choice. I also used this opportunity to seek feedback about the strengths and weaknesses of student affairs. At the end of the process, I emerged with a comprehensive picture of how the division was perceived (unevenly), its strengths and vulnerabilities (lots of both), whether the division was understood (mostly not), and how I might approach my first 6–12 months on the job.

Being an internal hire was an advantage in many ways. When you are hired from within, you have a chance to hit the ground running. Because relationships are already in place, there is less of a learning curve. I heard myself saying this during my interviews, and it was true. As an insider, I had an intimate perspective on the institution and the division. As vice president, I would have the advantage of working with colleagues I already knew well, and I was in a position to accelerate initiatives. As vice president, I would be able to continue conversations with the benefit of depth and context, which would save time.

The situation would have unfolded differently if I had been an outsider, without the benefit of existing relationships and the presumption of a certain level of background knowledge. But in some ways, my insider status worked against me. For example, after I became vice president, I reconfigured the division budget office, which was in disarray and a major vulnerability. During the realignment, I was short-staffed for a few months and secured budget support from the central budget office. Meanwhile, the university budget planning timeline proceeded normally and I participated at a significant disadvantage, as I was in the middle of a complete reorganization and did not have a senior budget officer. While the central budget office was supportive and accommodating, it was limited in the support it could provide at the division level. Had I been an external candidate, I might have pushed for a grace period until my budget office was up and running. As a division veteran, I did not feel that I had that option, in part because I did not want to negatively impact the work and progress of my colleagues in the budget office. I was disadvantaged from being able to advocate effectively for the needs of the division, because I inherited a budget office that needed a complete overhaul.

There are several tricky aspects of being hired from within. First, people tend to assume that you have a certain level of familiarity or knowledge. Internal hires have to speak up when they need more information and background to make decisions about an issue. An even bigger challenge is that everything an internal hire changes can be interpreted as a reflection on his or her predecessor. Although this may be the case in some situations, just because you make a change does not necessarily mean that things were broken before. Finally, there may be a disconnect between the internal hire's understanding of a situation and what actually took place, depending on how much information he or she had access to previously. As associate vice president, I was not privy to a lot of information that was discussed among executive officers; when I became vice president, my colleagues tended to assume that I knew more than I did about many issues. The theme here is access to information. Even if internal hires have been working in a highly collaborative environment, the transition into a senior-level position grants access to information they did not previously have. I found myself speed-reading everything I could and attending every possible meeting to catch up and get on a level playing field with my colleagues.

Start-up, Turnaround, Realignment, and Sustaining Success

Pros and cons of being the internal candidate are most likely to present themselves when it comes to analyzing the division and being able to move swiftly. My division was stable in certain areas and extremely fragile in others—probably a common experience for new vice presidents. Owing to my previous role as associate vice president, I had great transparency into the areas I formerly supervised and less expertise in the rest of the division. I needed to quickly assess all 20 departments and come up with a strategy to advance our priorities and get things done.

In *The First 90 Days*, Michael Watkins (2003) defined four categories of organizational condition: start-up, turnaround, realignment, and sustaining success.

> In a *start-up* you are charged with assembling the capabilities (people, funding, and technology) to get a new business, product, or project off the ground. In *turnaround* you take on a unit or group that is recognized to be in trouble and work to get it back on track. Both *start-ups* and *turnarounds* involve resource-intensive construction work—there isn't much existing infrastructure and capacity to build on. *Realignments* and *sustaining success*, by contrast, are situations that have significant strengths, but also serious constraints. In *realignment*, the challenge is to revitalize a unit that is drifting into trouble. In a *sustaining success* situation, you are preserving the vitality of a successful organization and taking it to the next level. (p. 61)

Across the division's 20 departments and approximately 350 staff members, it was easy to categorize all the programs and services according to Watkins' categories. I had a fairly even distribution across sustaining success, turnaround, and realignments, and I had at least two start-ups. I understood the division's strengths and vulnerabilities from my own experience and from the conversations I had both before and during the interview process. One of the reasons I applied for the vice president position was because I knew I would be able to make swift and lasting changes that would enable the division to thrive.

When I first arrived, the university was at a fascinating moment in time during which it was transforming and reconceptualizing the campus and student life experience. Colleges and universities are often criticized for moving at a glacial speed, so the opportunity to be involved in institutional decision making, culture change, and programmatic growth was exciting. I was aware that the campus and student life experience had been neglected for many years; the division had been engaged in many purposeful initiatives over the preceding decade, but it still had a ways to go. It was clear that student affairs had not been changing at the same velocity as the rest of the institution, and we had some catching up to do.

Being the Vice President

In the exploration phase of the vice presidential opportunity, I had many private conversations and public inquiries about my intentions. Once I decided to apply, I considered every day to be another day of interviews, and I did my best to remain authentic. Colleagues were genuinely respectful of the awkwardness that inevitably cropped up because my staff, colleagues, and trustees were involved in the recruitment and selection process. It was important that I maintain complete professionalism and make it clear that my candidacy was separate from my daily work. While it was nerve-wracking to be an internal candidate, I tried to maintain a confident outward appearance.

Unlike the transition to associate vice president, the appointment as vice president required that I purposefully think about how I would mark the transition, both physically and intellectually. The way I approached my old job would not work in the new one: I needed to operate at a higher strategic level and get out of the tactical weeds. The fact that I was staying at the same institution, had the same commute, and was going to the same suite (albeit a different office) every day could be a liability. In my case, it was important to have physical separation between my old and new jobs. I took a brief vacation to focus on the skills I needed for the new job. I was already a strong and decisive manager, and I knew my portfolio in depth. I needed time to consider how I would transition to spending less time managing and more time leading. To advance divisional and university priorities, I would need time and space to think strategically. Although I was able to take only a short week off, it was important to my transition and allowed me to begin to change my way of thinking.

Being an internal hire was both a blessing and a curse when it came to transitioning from my former job. I chose not to immediately fill my former position and, instead, moved ahead with other crucial hires to expedite division stability. I had not decided whether to keep the division structure the same, so it did not make sense to rush to fill my old job, especially as it contained the portfolio I was most knowledgeable about. This decision made sense to me, but it also created some challenges as I tried to transition out of my old role and into my new one. Had I immediately filled my old job, I could have directed people to the new person and more easily disassociated myself from the position.

Relationships Will Change Because You Will Change

New vice presidents have to be prepared to experience a tremendous personal and professional transition in full view of everyone. The position requires confidence, grace, humility, and self-awareness. I had to be conscious about which conversations and decisions I participated in and where I needed to step away and let my staff do their jobs. Shortly after I became vice president, my team was working through a problem that had arisen with an event they were planning with colleagues from across campus. As they ironed out the problem, they copied me on a series of e-mails that were also copied to the entire event planning staff. My staff copied me because they were used to doing so when I was associate vice president. However, the people they were writing to assumed that my staff members were intentionally elevating the matter, so they copied their vice president on their reply, which caused him to get involved unnecessarily. New vice presidents have to change in expected and unexpected ways. The vice president should no longer participate in some committees and conversations; this was hard for me, because I enjoyed being engaged, and the division was still in transition.

Velocity, Velocity, Velocity

New vice presidents—whether internal or external hires—might face a division that is not organized in a manner that allows them to make progress and achieve their objectives. In my case, the division was far from where I needed it to be and where I knew it had the greatest potential to affect students and advance university priorities. Within days of stepping into the role, I posted a new position, moved a couple staff members out, and realigned the division. Internal hires have built-in credibility and more flexibility than external hires to push hard and fast on issues. In fact, internal hires are expected to move with greater velocity, because they are familiar with the organization and do not need time to get up to speed.

These assumptions were tested in my first year and proved true time and time again. In the midst of all this activity, it was important for me to keep my finger on the pulse of the division and calibrate how much change the organization could tolerate at one time. I could assess my 20 departments and prioritize how I would make programmatic improvements and organizational changes. While some of the changes might have felt too fast, I am confident that we are headed in the right direction and that I am moving quickly where it is appropriate and more slowly where that is appropriate.

Chapter Summary

A few times in our lives we simply have to take the plunge when opportunity arises. For me, the chance to become vice president of student affairs was one of those times. In transitioning to this position as an internal candidate, I felt empowered and confident, but also vulnerable and full of self-doubt. The opportunity to advance important university priorities as an associate vice president had helped me learn more about my strengths, limitations, vulnerabilities, and fears. These experiences made me a better leader.

- Be open to new opportunities. The chance to step into a vice presidency as an internal candidate will not necessarily come at the most opportune time. Often these opportunities come when candidates think they are not prepared or not ready to take the next step. You might have many doubts about whether you are qualified for the job and whether the risk of not being selected is worth the exposure. Be open to these opportunities when they arise.

- Seek advice from friends. If you are ever considering becoming an internal candidate for a vice presidency, seek advice from trusted colleagues and friends. They can see your blind spots, and they will have their own perspective on your chances as a candidate and possible fallout. Colleagues and friends can help you assess the situation from perspectives you might not be able to see. Their responses may vary, but their opinions are important to consider.

- Think through all the possible outcomes. In the best case scenario, the internal candidate gets the job; in the worst case scenario, he or she does not get the job. For an internal candidate, not getting the job can be emotionally devastating and damaging to the candidate's reputation. You might believe that the only way to resolve this situation is to leave the institution. Even if you do get the job, you will face many challenges, such as how fast to move, how to make the transition from colleague to supervisor, and how to transition out of the old job and into the new job.

- Mark the transition. It is easy for internal candidates to remain stuck in old patterns of behavior, but if you do this, others will not treat you like the vice president for student affairs and you will not have the momentum you need to advance the division. Mark the transition physically by moving to the new office and intellectually by thinking more broadly about the entire institution rather than just the division.

Ⓣ Internal hires have built-in credibility and flexibility; they can push harder and faster on issues than external hires can. Be thoughtful about how you are going to use this power to get things done. At the same time, internal hires are often expected to move with greater velocity because they are more familiar with the organization and do not need time to get up to speed.

Reference

Watkins, M. (2003). *The first 90 days: Critical success strategies for new leaders at all levels*. Boston, MA: Harvard Business Review Press.

CHAPTER 5

Communication
The Most Overlooked Skill

Gage E. Paine

During the transition period, the need for information intensifies, making it critical for new vice presidents to pay attention to their communication strategies from the beginning. It is never too early to think about what you want to communicate and how you can be effective in your communication efforts. In this chapter, an experienced vice president for student affairs offers guidelines for how you can be thoughtful and strategic about your communications, both formal and informal, online and in person. Remember: Every word and action of a new vice president can affect the success of the transition.

As I was leaving my position of vice president for student affairs at the University of Texas at San Antonio, I learned about a rumor that circulated before I started that job—that I did not like open-toed shoes. I have no idea how that rumor started—I never discussed shoes in my interviews and I do not have an opinion on open-toed shoes—but it is a great example of an important point for leaders to remember. Well-known management consultant Meg Wheatley (2006) put it this way:

Everybody needs information to do their work. We are so needy of this resource that if we can't get the real thing, we make it up. When rumors proliferate and gossip gets out of hand, it is always a sign that people lack the genuine article—honest, meaningful information. Given that we all need to be nourished by information, it is no wonder that employees cite "poor communication" as one of their greatest problems. People know it is critical to their ability to do good work. They know when they are starving. (p. 99)

If you have been selected as a vice president for student affairs, you have been successful at communicating on some level. You have successfully completed a complex series of interviews, have been effective in multiple positions, and have shown yourself to be a leader. You are likely to feel confident about your communication skills. However, during a transition, the need for information intensifies, making it critical for new vice presidents to pay attention to their communication strategies from the beginning. It is never too early to think about what you want to communicate and how you can be effective in your communication efforts. Your strategy begins with your interviews and continues through each interaction with colleagues at your new university. Conversely, if you are already serving as a vice president, it is not too late to become a strategic communicator. Being thoughtful about how and what you communicate is an important skill in the transition process and throughout your career.

Everything Communicates Something

It is not possible to control what people say and think, but you can manage what you say and do. Parker J. Palmer (2000) described it best: "I . . . have come to understand that for better or worse, I lead by word and deed *simply because I am here doing what I do.* If you are also here, doing what you do, then you also exercise leadership of some sort" (p. 74). Assuming a new position is the closest we will ever come to starting with a blank slate. Of course, it is not completely blank, because your reputation will precede you. But even though new colleagues will gather information from the Internet and reference checks, you still have a chance to start relationships afresh. Be aware that you send messages with every word and every action; just doing what you do every day will set a tone. What is important to you? What ideas do you want to communicate? How will you communicate them? What kind of leadership will you exercise?

Everyone is paying attention to the new vice president, to what you say and do. You are a role model; this is part of the job. People know in a general way what you do, but everything about you will be noticed now. They will look for meaning in everything you say and do. If you have ever spent much time around small children, you may have noticed that they are like tape recorders. Sometimes it is a shock to hear adult words coming out of their mouths. They even mimic the inflection perfectly. Colleagues and staff will pay attention as closely as that small child to your words and actions. Unfortunately, they rarely are as accurate as tape recorders, so you have to be as clear and consistent as possible. There will be specific messages you want everyone to hear and messages that need to be different for different audiences. Spend time interacting with your new colleagues, identifying the messages and ideas you want to share, and thinking about ways to share them consistently. One important reality: New colleagues will remember with pinpoint accuracy where your words and actions are not in alignment. Everything you say and do communicates something.

People Want to Know What You Care About

Beginning with the interview, focus on being yourself. Answer questions honestly and thoughtfully, and ask questions about issues you care about; both behaviors communicate who you are. Present an accurate picture, and promise only what you can deliver. When you arrive on campus, find ways to share information about your expectations as soon as you can. Not everyone has had the same experiences you have had; therefore, you cannot expect everyone to be working from the same assumptions. I learned this in one of my first supervisory positions. It did not occur to me that I needed to tell a new staff member not to take nonemergency personal calls during a student conduct interview, but he needed that guidance from me. You may feel as though you are talking down to people when you state expectations as basic and simple as this example, but members of the division want to know what you expect. They want to know your priorities and what you value; clarity helps avoid misunderstandings.

When I take a new leadership position, I hold an all-staff meeting as soon as possible. At Trinity University, I met with everyone in one meeting. At The University of Texas at San Antonio and The University of Texas at Austin, the student affairs divisions were so large that we held multiple meetings so every staff member could attend. In each case, I made a few remarks about my values and expectations, then opened the floor for questions. I let people know that I am willing to be asked any question, including questions that were not asked during my interview. The following are some of the general expectations I discuss at the first all-staff meeting:

- The students. All jobs in student affairs have the same underlying purpose—to do the best we can for students and the university community—regardless of our titles. We are in service to students. It is always about students' experience, and we should always treat them with respect.
- Work collaboratively, not competitively. Squares on the organization chart help us organize our work, but they should not be used to box us in or keep us from working together.
- We will be ethical and follow university procedures. Bureaucracy is an aid to our work, not its purpose or a hindrance. We work with university procedures to find ways to say "yes" to students, and we take the time to explain when we have to say "no."
- We respect everyone. We respect each other and each student, finding time to listen and explain. We work to be fair and consistent, and to treat each person as an individual.
- We should be engaged on campus. Know what is going on and what students care about. Read the campus newspaper regularly and participate in division and university programs. Be a part of

the community. This will increase your ability to get things done. The more you know, the more effective you will be in your role and the more you can help students be effective.

The question and answer process may feel risky, but it is worth the risk. It is the first step toward communicating openness to staff input. I have never had anyone ask an inappropriate question, and the questions are often the first sign of issues of concern. I have been asked about books I like to read, pets, and hobbies, all of which contribute to a sense that I am a normal person just like everyone else.

Your Presence Is a Communication Tool

An interesting thing about interviewing is that you are asked questions you are not asked in any other setting, and you can learn from your answers. In one interview, I heard myself saying something I have said many times since: "My job is to handle the administrative parts of the position well enough that I have time to engage with students." I have grown to understand that I also need to find time to engage staff and colleagues. As a new vice president, you will have an overwhelming amount of information to absorb and a constant stream of people who want to meet you. Where should you spend your time? What events should you attend? What messages are communicated by your presence or absence? A huge part of the vice president position is face time—time you spend being visible to and interacting with others. Students, staff, and faculty appreciate your presence.

One strategy I use in my first year in a new job is to attend everything I am invited to. It makes the year extremely busy, but it sends the message that I am willing to be involved in the life and work of the campus community. Attending so many programs and events early on helps in two ways: (1) It allows me to make better decisions about where to invest my time in the future, and (2) it builds a perception that I am accessible. The first year on the job is the most important year in terms of accessibility; if people perceive you as not available in that first year, it is almost impossible to undo that reputation.

As I met with student groups when I started at The University of Texas at Austin, I told them, "I want to meet all 50,000 students." It was always good for a laugh, but it also communicated an important idea: Students are important to me and I want to meet them. I asked each group to help me achieve my goal by inviting me to the meetings of their other organizations. As a result, I met with a wide variety of groups in a short period and learned what students were concerned about. This way I was not surprised when issues emerged, and I could appropriately advise university leadership.

New vice presidents communicate messages with other actions as well. Who do you meet with in the first few weeks? Equally important, who are you *not* meeting with? People pay attention to both. Have a plan and let people know the plan, so groups understand that they are not being forgotten. I have found that most people understand that you will not be able to get to everyone in the first weeks and are understanding if they know they will have your attention in the near future.

E-mail is another important messaging medium—not so much the content of the e-mails but the use of e-mail as a communication strategy. Do you support family life for staff? Do you tell people that work/life balance is important? If you are sending e-mails to staff members at 2:00 a.m., you are communicating the opposite message. (If your best work time is in the early hours of the morning, I suggest that you save the e-mail drafts and send them later from the office.) Obviously, we all have our work schedules and styles, but as vice president you run the risk of imposing your style on others if you are not paying attention. We also need to pay attention to the way our actions match our styles, and simple things like e-mail can trip us up.

Learn as Much as Possible as Quickly as Possible

When I arrived at The University of Texas at San Antonio, the vice presidency had been vacant for nearly a year and a half. A number of things were on hold, waiting for the new vice president to be part of the decision process. Six months into the job I was asked, "What was your biggest surprise?" My answer: "The number of decisions I had to make in the first month with little information." My advice is to learn as much as possible as quickly as you can. You never know when a critical issue or opportunity will land on your desk and require an immediate decision. All your actions communicate your priorities and all of them will be understood in the context of the institution. One way to ensure that you are being heard in the way you intend is to make an effort to understand as much as you can about your new institution.

New vice presidents need to meet with certain groups as soon as possible. I met with each department in the division as soon as the time could be scheduled. I asked each department head to set the agenda and decide who should attend. I let them know that I trusted them regarding what was important to their departments and what to share with me at the first meeting. This approach communicates two messages: (1) You want to learn about them rather than assuming you know their issues and concerns, and (2) you trust them to tell you what is important. There will be time later to dig deeper—the initial meeting allows them to decide what to discuss and how to present it.

Additional groups to meet include your vice presidential colleagues, student leaders, your predecessor (if appropriate), chairs of faculty and staff councils, academic deans, vice provosts who interact with student affairs, key leaders on your campus, and key faculty members. Meeting with this diverse group of people gives you an opportunity to learn about the university community. And do not assume that you are aware of everyone you should meet; some constituencies are obvious, but it is helpful to ask division leaders, search committee members, and the president for lists of people you should meet. The lists will vary depending on campus, culture, and situation. For example, at The University of Texas at Austin, my list included several former student leaders. This makes sense, but it was not considered important at either of the other campuses where I had served as a vice president. If I had relied on my experience and not asked for advice from campus leaders, I would have omitted this group and, in doing so, communicated an indifference I did not feel.

Read everything you can get your hands on—at least give it a thorough skim. Read the student paper every day. Know the institutional values and read the strategic plan. Visit the web pages of all departments in the student affairs division. Do the same for the websites of all colleges and schools at the university; focus on trying to understand what they value and how your division can help. Seek information in traditional ways (e.g., bulletins, brochures, websites) and nontraditional ways (e.g., conference presentations, Facebook, Twitter, dean's retreat). The sooner you understand the priorities and concerns of the university, the better decisions you will make from the start, the better you will navigate the challenges of the new position, and the more effective your communication efforts will be.

Ask Good Questions

Someone explained to me that the questions we ask define the answers we receive. I came to understand this more clearly when I worked in services for students with disabilities just as the Americans with Disabilities Act of 1990 was being enacted. As we worked with professors to make accommodations for students, I realized that for most faculty members the underlying question was "How do I test this student in a way that is most like the way I test everyone else?" I eventually realized that the question we should be asking was "How do I test this person in a way that allows me to understand what he or she has learned?" These two questions elicit different kinds of answers. This was an important lesson that has affected my entire career—I always try to ask the best questions I can.

One of the prime opportunities as a new vice president is to ask questions, lots of questions. You are not expected to know things, and your job is to ask questions. You have a chance to ask why things are the way they are. The original reason is often lost in history, or circumstances have changed but the program or service has not. Being new, you can ask students, non-student-affairs staff, and faculty questions about the division without much risk; they do not have to worry about offending you, because you did not develop these programs. As you become more deeply connected with the division, people may become more hesitant to tell you the truth and more afraid of offending you, because the programs and services will be identified with you. Ask questions from multiple perspectives. The questions themselves define the set of possible answers, so be creative in your questions and listen for creative answers. Be careful not to make assumptions. Do not ask questions that are too narrow; ask open-ended questions and questions that will help you understand issues in enough detail. Ask the same questions of multiple groups, and look for themes in responses. Pay attention to the mix of topics and the kinds of questions you ask. Ask tough questions as soon as you can, and listen carefully to the answers.

When I meet with a group and people seem reticent to start asking questions or volunteering information, I ask these two questions: What do you love about the university? What would you change? I take parking off the table. It is too easy to complain about and I cannot fix it. That generally gets a laugh, which lightens the mood. It is wonderful to hear people talk about what they love about the community, and responses to the change question provide insight into concerns. Answering the second question might seem risky, but as a newcomer you are not seen as part of the problem, so most people feel free to answer. Also, as a newcomer, it is fine if you do not have a solution or understand the background; your lack of knowledge gives you freedom to investigate.

Listening as a Communication Tool

Wheatley (2002) noted that "we can change the world if we start listening to one another again. Simple, honest, human conversation. Not mediation, negotiation, problem-solving, debate, or public meetings. Simple, truthful conversation where we each have a chance to speak, we each feel heard and we each listen well" (p. 2).

Listening may be the most powerful tool a new vice president has. Listen to everyone who wants to talk with you. As you ask questions, show that you are listening in all the ways we know already: follow up with questions, add comments, nod your head, lean forward. Listening communicates to people that you truly do want to hear the good and the bad information. Find ways to listen to people who rarely get a chance to talk with the vice president. I read this idea in a leadership newsletter: Ask for a list of the entire division sorted by birthday month, then invite everyone who has a birthday that month to join you for a conversation and light snacks. This brings together a diverse group of people from across the division who get to meet some colleagues for the first time and have a chance to visit with the new vice president. This monthly conversation has enabled me to meet individually and talk with more members of the housing facilities and food staffs than I otherwise would have.

People want to hear from the new vice president. They want to learn about you. They ask you questions, and they want you to give them answers. They want to learn from you—this is important, but it is more important that you learn from them. To accomplish this, you must learn to be silent and create a space that invites others to speak about what is important to them. Can you sit in silence long enough to allow others in the room to think of a question, to feel safe enough to tell a difficult truth from their perspectives? Finding the balance between talking and listening is an essential skill for a leader in transition. It is incredibly challenging and should be a priority.

Use a Variety of Communication Resources

Inventory and evaluate the communication tools used by the division. What does the website look like, and is it easy to navigate? What messages does it communicate? What are the internal communication methods? How are social media used? Are the communication tools effective, or do they need improvement? What is missing and needs to be created?

Your selection as vice president for student affairs implies that you have a history of effectively communicating, but stepping into this role is different from other transitions you have made. Trust in your experience, but take the time to be thoughtful and strategic about your communications, both formal and informal, online and in person.

Newsletters

When I began at The University of Texas at San Antonio, the Division of Student Affairs had a biweekly staff newsletter. I was asked to write an essay introducing myself. Two weeks later, I wrote about the university's strategic planning process and our role in it. Two weeks after that, there was something else I wanted to inform the division about. Before I knew it, I was writing regularly for the staff newsletter. I came to understand how effective this was as a communication tool—it allowed me to share important messages and enabled people to get to know me and the issues I cared about.

When I started at The University of Texas at Austin, there was no staff newsletter. During the interview process I had learned that the division needed better mechanisms for internal communication, so even before I started the job I worked with the director of communications, and the first staff e-newsletter was sent out shortly after I started. It has helped me communicate across a large division and has given our departments a way to brag and share information. The newsletter supports the work of the departments and has helped me convey messages about the importance of shared information and collaboration. A colleague at another institution uses a newsletter to demonstrate the value of the division of student affairs and communicate about its programs to deans and faculty members. We are considering this idea, as well as the idea of using an e-newsletter, to reconnect with alumni and donors.

Facebook

Originally, I had to be convinced that social media were worth my time. I was involved with the Southern Association for College Student Affairs and National Association of Student Personnel Administrators Region III New Professionals Institute for 6 years. During the first 5 years, we set up electronic mailing lists so participants could keep in touch. In the 6th year, a participant set up a Facebook page, which I reluctantly joined. To my surprise, I enjoyed it; I reconnected with friends from college, former staff, and former students. Then a student "friended" me, and I had to make a decision about my response. I received contradictory advice from a number of friends and colleagues about how to respond when students friend the vice president on Facebook. Ultimately, I decided that if I was going to get involved with social media, I needed to fully engage, so I accepted the friend request. My personal policy since then has been to accept friend requests but never ask to friend students or staff members. As students started becoming my Facebook friends, I realized an enormous professional benefit—gaining a window on student life that I would not have found any other way. Occasionally I read about a concern and can share resources with students. I do not troll looking for issues, but if a student shares something that is a concern or a possible rule violation, I notify the appropriate person. I am comfortable with this practice because the students are the ones who asked to connect with me.

Twitter

At the 2011 NASPA Annual Conference, I heard a lot of discussion about Twitter. Until then, I had not been willing to try it. Most students I talked to did not use it. However, after the conference, I decided that I needed to at least learn about it. So I set up a Twitter account and dove in. At first, it was helpful as a connection to professional colleagues and a new way to find (way too many) articles to read. Students at the University of Texas at San Antonio were not using Twitter much at that time. When I changed campuses, my use changed. Fewer students at my new campus friend me on Facebook, but I created a new Twitter account and have significantly more followers in a few months than I did in more than a year at the previous campus—many of them students and alumni. Being on Twitter has helped me connect with students. Their reaction has been very positive, including a front-page article in the campus newspaper and being listed as one of the top 10 university Twitter accounts to follow.

We use both Facebook and Twitter strategically in the Division of Student Affairs at The University of Texas at Austin. We take photos at every division event and post them on Facebook and Twitter. This drives more traffic to the Facebook page, as people tag themselves and find friends or colleagues in the photographs. As with the newsletter, this exposure enables a wider range of people to know more about what we are doing in student affairs. We have also developed a social media campaign to help me meet new students. About every other week, I schedule 30 minutes at various campus locations to talk with any student who shows up. This initiative works on multiple levels. First, I have the opportunity to meet with students I would not have met otherwise. Second, even if students choose not to come meet with me, thanks to the multiplicative effect of tweets and retweets by departments, students, and staff, students all across campus know that I am making an effort to reach out. In a short time, this initiative has given me a reputation for being accessible and willing to engage students. Most important, I have had some great discussions with the students who show up. I have found technology to be a more effective way to facilitate face-to-face interactions than I would ever have expected.

Find Your Voice

You can use all these communication methods to get your voice out to the division and the campus. No matter what kind of leadership role you have held before, you have probably been implementing someone else's vision. At the vice presidential level, you will be implementing the president's vision, but you will also have the opportunity to implement your own vision for the division of student affairs. You might think it takes time to develop a vision in a new job, but I have come to understand vision on a number of levels. As I understand it, I have something to share with the organization from the very beginning. I do not have a vision for the individual departments in the division; I rely on the leadership of each department to tell me what is needed for them to be the best. But I do have a clear overall vision about why we do the work we do and how we should work together, and that is my voice as vice president.

I repeatedly share messages about being student-focused, about the importance of communication, about ethics, and about being partners with faculty and staff in other divisions. I use the newsletter, social media, meetings, and so on to share these messages in multiple ways. I believe that my messages and actions come together to create my voice.

In my first job as a vice president, I followed someone who had been a strong presence for many years on that campus. In that situation, I was intentional in not being the first voice to be heard in a meeting. It's a practice I continue to this day, because if the vice president speaks first, many people think the discussion is over. I might have carried it too far, because some people felt that something was missing—my voice. I have become a little quicker to contribute, although I still try not to be the first voice if possible. But meetings and discussions are not the only place for a vice president's voice to be heard, which is why I use multiple methods to make sure important messages are heard throughout the division.

You Will Make Mistakes

Mistakes come in all sizes and levels of importance. The hard reality is that you will make some. In my first year at Trinity University, I was charged with leading a committee on the quality of student life. At the end of our deliberations, we submitted recommendations to the president. He was not impressed. Ultimately, he accepted the report and we used it as our guidelines for significant change over the next 6 years, but we got off to a rough start because I had not given him what he wanted. I had not asked enough questions and had made some assumptions; I thought I knew what I was doing, but I did not have a clear picture of the end result he wanted.

A colleague told me a great story about a term—*water carrier*—that he picked up from a book he had read. He used the phrase in a speech to praise employees who had gone the extra mile in the division of student affairs, but no one in the audience had read the book and he had not told enough of the story to provide context. For some people the term was confusing, for others, vaguely insulting. After the speech, my colleague was approached by a member of the custodial staff who shared his concern about the term as it had been applied to him. At this point, he realized that the term could be insulting if not properly explained. Remember, you do not share a history with your new colleagues, so they will not know what you are talking about unless you provide sufficient context. In the tradition of first impressions, everything you say during the early months will count more than what you say later, once they get to know you. You have not developed a trust relationship yet, so you do not have much room for error. Think before you speak.

Do Not Be Afraid to Say the Most Important Words

A staff member once told me he was surprised and impressed to hear me say "I don't know" in response to a question at my first student government meeting. He had learned somewhere along the way that it was not a good strategy to use those words. While there may be places where that is not a good strategy, it has always seemed to me better not to try to fake an answer when I do not really have one. But after I admitted that I did not know the answer, I followed up with another important statement: "I'll learn more about it." Be honest.

As we all learned early in life, "please" and "thank you" are important words. Let people know you appreciate their assistance as you get acclimated. Acknowledge that you need their help to be successful, and do not hesitate to express your gratitude publicly. Ultimately, this is the most important communication task of any leader, and it is critical for your new role as vice president.

On the Leadership Challenge website, Jim Kouzes and Barry Posner (2003) wrote:

> [A]t the heart of leadership is caring. Without caring, leadership has no purpose. And without showing others that you care and what you care about, other people won't care about what you say or what you know. . . . When leaders commend individuals for achieving the values or goals of the organiza-

tion, they give them courage, inspiring them to experience their own ability to deliver—even when the pressure is on. When we recognize women and men for their contributions, we expand their awareness of their value to the organization and to their co-workers. (para. 2–4)

Chapter Summary

Communication is the most overlooked strategy in transition planning for a new vice presidency. Too often this skill is taken for granted because we are constantly communicating, but every word and action of a new vice president can affect the success of the transition.

- You send a message with every word and every action; just doing what you do every day sets a tone. Everyone is paying attention. You are a role model and this is part of the job. You will be surprised at how much people notice and what they read into everything you say and do.

- As soon as possible, create venues to share your expectations. Everyone has had different experiences, so you cannot expect everyone to be working from the same assumptions. People want to know what you care about; reflect on it and take every opportunity to share that message.

- Attend everything you are invited to in the first year. It makes the year extremely busy, but it sends the message that you are willing to be involved in the campus community. Attending so many programs and events early on will help you (1) make better decisions about where to invest your time in the future and (2) build the perception that you are accessible. The first year on the job is the most important year in terms of accessibility; if people perceive you as not available in that first year, it is almost impossible to undo that reputation.

🛈 Learn as much as possible as quickly as you can. You never know when a critical issue or opportunity will appear on your desk and require a quick decision. One way to ensure that you are being heard in the way you intend is to be sure you understand as much as possible about your new university.

🛈 As a new vice president, ask questions, lots of questions. You are not expected to know things, and your job is to ask questions. You have a chance to ask why things are the way they are. The original reason is often lost in history or circumstances have changed, but the program or service has not. Because you are new, you can ask questions about the division without much risk; take advantage of this freedom.

🛈 Listening may be the most powerful tool a new vice president has. Listen to everyone who wants to talk with you. As you ask questions, show that you are listening in all the ways we know: follow up with questions, add comments, nod your head, lean forward. Listening communicates to people that you want to hear the good and the bad. Find ways to listen to people who rarely get a chance to talk with the vice president.

🛈 Be thoughtful and strategic about your communications, both formal and informal, online and in person. Use newsletters, e-mail, Facebook, Twitter, and other communication tools to get your message out. Your audience is evolving and you should as well.

🛈 Do not be afraid to say "I don't know." While there may be places where that is not a good strategy, it is better not to try to fake an answer when you do not have one. You are not expected to have answers for everything during your transition into the job. There will be numerous issues and challenges you have not had time to think through and for which you have not yet developed a competent response.

References

Kouzes, J., & Posner, B. (2003). *Encouraging the heart.* Retrieved from http://www.leadershipchallenge.com/Leaders-Section-Articles-Stories-Detail/encouraging-the-heart.aspx

Palmer, P. J. (2000). *Let your life speak: Listening for the voice of vocation.* San Francisco, CA: Jossey-Bass.

Wheatley, M. (2002). *Turning to one another: Simple conversations to restore hope to the future.* San Francisco, CA: Berrett-Koehler.

Wheatley, M. (2006). *Leadership and the new science: Discovering order in a chaotic world* (3rd ed.). San Francisco, CA: Berrett-Koehler.

CHAPTER 6

Strategies for Success and Pitfalls to Avoid

John R. Laws

With the executive shortage, opportunities exist for aspiring leaders to fill those roles. But once an executive administrator is hired, his or her performance is closely watched and evaluated. How can a student affairs professional successfully move into a new leadership role? In this chapter, the author identifies strategies and provides insights that will help the new vice president for student affairs build a strong foundation. But these strategies will be meaningless if you do not avoid common pitfalls such as lack of a plan, vague expectations, not respecting the culture, not setting the right tone, making changes too fast, and not working with an institutional mentor.

Higher education is experiencing an executive shortage, with vacancies in senior administrative positions at many institutions. Basic demographics are affecting the workforce as college and university leaders retire, and younger generations are not filling these leadership positions in sufficient numbers. The changing nature of the leadership positions, increased personal obligations, and shifting interests of potential executives have resulted in fewer qualified applicants for open positions (Mead-Fox, 2009). For all of these reasons, the odds that a president will fail or will step down earlier than expected are higher than ever before.

Still, the daunting challenges do not mean that leadership positions cannot be filled successfully. A small cadre of strong and increasingly diverse leaders is on the way up. The compensation and stature of these positions continue to be a draw (Mead-Fox, 2009). If well prepared, new leaders can be successful and provide needed leadership to their institution.

Setting the tone early and correctly is critical for the short- and long-term success of the new vice president and the organization. New vice presidents must be intentional about the path they take toward future achievement. The transition into an executive position requires time and planning, and should be phased in, with milestones and measurable outcomes. Change management works best when it is planned and executed over a 1- to 3-year period (MindTools, n.d.).

Preparing for the New Role

Candidates for the position of vice president for student affairs must do their homework. In preparing for the interview process, they should conduct serious research into the institution's mission, values, and vision. Missions vary significantly among community colleges and 4-year institutions, public and private schools, and other institution types. Candidates should review the institution's vision statement and strategic plan to develop a thorough understanding of the mission and how it is executed by the administration. Studying the organization chart is also helpful to gain knowledge of institutional operations and structure.

Once you are selected as the new vice president, make it a priority to meet with the administrative assistant. Begin developing a work relationship with this person and ask for assistance. The administrative assistant should ensure that everything is set up for you to be productive on the first day. Necessary items include a computer, system log-in, e-mail address, business cards, parking pass, keys, telephone, and name tag. Institutional policy might prevent some items from being available immediately, but the necessary paperwork should be completed on the first day.

Inquire about press releases and other strategies to announce your arrival at the institution and in the community. A formal announcement will raise awareness that the division is under new leadership. It should include details about your previous positions and how that experience will benefit the institution. Make sure the press release highlights mission-specific experience at your former institution, so stakeholders will see how that experience meshes with the responsibilities of your new position. The press is not the most important recipient of this release; donors, board members, new colleagues, peers at other institutions, and business leaders will appreciate the information, which will prime them to work with you. To facilitate the preparation of the press release, be prepared with a professional photograph and an updated biography.

People tend to put too much pressure on themselves in a new job, imposing high expectations from the first day. No one, including the president, expects a new vice president to solve major problems right away. Instead, look for small, early wins to establish credibility and build support within the institutional community. By carefully planning and executing a transition strategy, you can be effective, demonstrate competency, and progress in the role. Use trusted friends and colleagues as mentors, sounding boards, confidantes, and devil's advocates. These trusted peers are essential to your professional development and success as you change roles or face difficult decisions. Starting a new job can be both exciting and overwhelming; colleagues and friends can ease the transition and provide strategies and perspective on the opportunity.

Building Relationships Early

One of the most important tasks for a new employee is to develop relationships. Professionally fulfilling, respectful, and caring relationships take time to evolve; the new vice president should begin working on them early. Build relationships by easing tensions and sharing personal priorities. Sharing will pay major dividends as you begin developing your team. Be self-confident, strategic, decisive, and assertive, and help build confidence across the institution (Hewlett, Leader-Chivée, Sherbin, Gordon, & Dieudonné, 2012). People will be watching, assessing, and learning from your example. Students, staff, colleagues, members of the public, and others will all have different expectations for you than they have for lower level staff. It is essential to set a tone that is appropriate for the college, the division, and yourself.

The President

Your first meeting should be with the president, if possible. This meeting will continue the relationship-building that began during the interview process and will help you establish expectations and direction. The meeting may be a simple welcome or more business-oriented, depending on the president's style. Be prepared for either. Try to identify key objectives, metrics, and any important projects or tasks for which you are responsible (RHR International, n.d.b). Ask about the frequency of future meetings and how to contact the president. Learn about his or her preferences and communication style. A frank discussion of the division's strengths and weaknesses should be part of these early conversations.

Ask the president whether there were internal candidates for the position and, if so, why they were not chosen. You need to know what the institution was looking for that these candidates did not offer. It is also helpful to know whether someone might be rankled and hoping that you fail. Ask about the decision to hire outside the institution. Inquire about an institutional mentor; some institutions have formal programs to pair new employees with a peer. If such a program is not in place, seek out this type of relationship on your own.

The Division and the Campus

Soon after you start the new job, have an all-staff meeting. Start the meeting by talking about your background, career experiences, and values, then move on to set initial expectations, describe your vision for student affairs, and begin building relationships. Employees will be interested to hear about their new boss's preferred ways of interacting and communicating (e.g., e-mail, voicemail, texting), and work habits. New vice presidents may also want to share personal information such as family details, recreational activities, and interests. Regarding the work itself, some vice presidents want to create a division that is strategic, proactive, creative, diverse, hardworking, performance-driven, results-oriented, and responsive to students. Others may articulate a different set of values. This is an opportunity to share your personal vision or a directive from the president. Clarify your expectations, stress your commitment to a positive attitude toward students, and share your enthusiasm for student services work (Clement & Rickard, 1992). The meeting should end with a question-and-answer session and an upbeat comment.

Make sure you are introduced to your colleagues and to key stakeholders (e.g., faculty, staff, students, community members). Invest time in meeting people and learning what they do and how they view student affairs. Learn what student affairs does well, how it can improve, and what your division can do to help others in their work. Get to know administrative support staff, custodians, and security personnel; these employees are often overlooked and underappreciated, but they have valuable insights into the people and functions of the institution. Embrace opportunities to visit with them.

Direct Reports

After introductions and settling in to the new campus, get to work learning more about the division and the staff. Review the biographies and résumés of your direct reports, and schedule meetings with them. Ask each person the same questions:

- How would you describe your job? Ask what they like most about the job, what they do not like, and how they spend their time. The answers to these questions could take time, especially if they include descriptions of major projects, but the time you spend listening is a good investment. This information will help you get up to speed quickly on the major issues in the division and the college.

- What are your professional goals? Ask this question after the first one. Ask them if their work is contributing to these goals or if their work is unrelated to what they ultimately want to do professionally.
- What does the division do well? Solicit insights from direct reports on the strengths of the division, so you can acknowledge them and build on them.
- What can the division do better? Staff responses to this question can provide ideas for the future, as well as insight into the needs of the division and people's willingness to change. Follow up by asking why needed changes have not been made.
- What advice do you have for me? Listen and thank them for their ideas. Do not refute any idea or opinion. Your staff members will appreciate the fact that you asked for their advice. Make it clear that you are collecting input and you appreciate theirs but that no decisions will be made too quickly.

Peers

Arrange to meet with your cabinet-level peers. These meetings will be an important first step in building the relationships and trust critical to long-term success. The meetings will probably last about an hour and should take place in their offices, which will allow you to observe clues (e.g., family and pet pictures, awards, souvenirs, mementos) that will help you connect. Ask about the following:

- Their objectives and challenges as they relate to student affairs.
- What student affairs can do to help their area be successful.
- What student affairs does well and what it can do better.
- Opinions and views of individuals in your division.
- The best way to communicate with the president and other peers.

- What the cabinet meetings are like and what is accomplished.
- How institutional problems are identified and analyzed, and how decisions are made.

Ask whether they had any issues with previous vice presidents of student affairs and what advice they might have for you as a new team member. Make it clear that you want and appreciate their help; people like being asked to help. Schedule regular meetings to get to know their values, goals, and interests. The president will ask your peers how the new vice president is doing, which makes it even more important to build these bridges. Personal interactions with your peers are perfectly acceptable; for example, house-hunting assistance, invitations to family dinners, and other forms of transition assistance.

Learning About the Institution

Every institution uses certain kinds of hardware, software, and management tools. Learn about these systems and how to use them. You should start getting log-in information, training on important systems, and access to student information immediately. Ask clerical support workers and others to help you with the learning curve so you can quickly achieve a basic understanding of student data, purchasing, and budget systems. Have a frank discussion with the director of human resources; discuss past performance appraisals, disciplinary issues, and staff turnover rates. Meet with the university finance officer to learn about the division's budget and fiscal areas of responsibility. Request reports on year-to-date spending and forecasted full-year spending; compare these spending patterns with benchmark data and past years' results. Ask about spending procedures, approval processes, levels of authority, and the rules for credit or purchasing cards.

As vice president, you may or may not have direct responsibility for enrollment management; clarify the expectations in this area. To some extent, all employees are responsible for supporting student retention, but you will need a clear understanding of your specific role in recruitment, retention, and completion. Few other issues affect the institution's mission, image, and finances as much as student enrollment does. Failure to understand the president's expectations of you in this area could be a fatal mistake.

Use data from reports to emphasize key points and make decisions. As vice president for student affairs, you must establish yourself as an expert on students and student issues. Your role in the institution is to understand students and their views. Make sure you know the demographic data, student characteristics, student concerns, and issues facing students. Use data and specific stories about students to advocate on their behalf. Gather information by attending student meetings and events, and dropping by student gathering spots. Be accessible to students so they will tell you what's going on. Focus on being a good listener and an advocate for student needs.

As the new vice president, you must find out which federal and state regulations and grants your division is responsible for monitoring and reporting (e.g., Family Educational Rights and Privacy Act [FERPA], Health Insurance Portability and Accountability Act of 1996 [HIPPA], Jeanne Clery Disclosure of Campus Security Policy and Campus Crime Statistics Act [Clery Act], Drug-Free Campus, TRIO grant, Perkins grant). At many institutions, the vice president for student affairs has some responsibility for compliance efforts related to federal and state regulations. Failure to understand this role could put an institution at risk. Find out who is responsible for maintaining federal compliance records, when reports are due, and who is responsible for submitting them. Federal regulation compliance is usually an unfamiliar area for a first-time vice president, and this topic is often overlooked when a new administrator arrives. Be sure all regulations are being met and that recordkeeping continues uninterrupted.

Establishing Direction

Deciding how best to move the division forward is a complex issue with multiple parts, some relevant and some irrelevant. In the transition period, the vice president needs to pay attention to the management team and establish shared values for working together. Opportunities exist in the first year to connect with colleagues at neighboring institutions and with members of the community who are invested in the institution. The first year is also important for establishing a critical business agenda for the future. Do not underestimate the value of regular meetings and communication with the division; they will enable you to assess how well your strategies are working. Make professional development a key tool for moving the division forward. We are only as good as the people we have developed.

The Team

After a few weeks, the new vice president should meet with his or her management team. This group—usually composed of direct reports—will be at the heart of implementing change and producing high-quality results. The first meeting should begin the process of molding this group of leaders into a cohesive, high-performing team. Plan for an extended meeting to ensure that you have uninterrupted time to discuss and process the tasks of working together as a team. The most important objective of the meeting is to determine what role the leadership team will play in the overall management of the division. Getting this role right is crucial to division performance and morale. Generally, the leadership team should be the decision-making body for major division issues, such as strategy, structure, staffing, succession planning, budgets, compensation, and culture. Individual circumstances and situations will vary, but a participatory, collaborative approach usually fits most circumstances. There will be times when you have to make unpopular decisions, but team members will be more engaged and committed if they are involved in important decisions.

Schedule meetings with other key employees in student affairs. Depending on the size of the staff and the available time, one-on-one meetings may not be possible, but they are preferred. These meetings can be a good way to connect with staff and to learn about them and the division. Use these meetings to validate information from other sources and to inquire about professional goals. Ask about their career goals, where they see themselves in 5 years, and how the division can help them do their work. Avoid making immediate promises, but assure them that their requests will be considered and reviewed. Ask them about their families, hobbies, and other interests, and what they like and do not like about work.

Avoid highly personal conversations. Although you want to start building rapport with staff members, be careful to minimize personal interactions that might compromise your ability to make decisions in the future. Employees eager to build relationships with the new boss may offer to host a dinner, assist in house-hunting, or conduct tours of the local schools and community. These offers should be respectfully declined. Business lunches are fine, but getting together with spouses or families can make later decisions more difficult. The new vice president needs to make any restructuring decisions on the basis of business factors only.

Shared Values

At the first staff meeting, outline the values of the student affairs division and clearly define associated positive and negative behaviors. Make sure that the team is aligned on these values and behaviors. The culture of a division stems from the collective values of its leadership and the acceptance of those values by the team. During the transition, the management team should agree on and be aligned with the values that will drive the division's future employment, performance, and compensation decisions.

Student learning outcomes and associated metrics offer strong direction for the team and can earn respect from the larger institution. By identifying and tracking specific and measurable outcomes, the division will be able to demonstrate the value it adds to the student experience and to implementation of the institution's mission. Establishing these metrics as a group will help all parties understand them and support their use.

Neighboring Institutions and Community Engagement

The new vice president should look to neighboring institutions. Identify individuals at neighboring institutions with whom you can interact, beginning with your counterpart. Introduce yourself, develop these relationships, and look for ways to collaborate. For example, identify collaborative staff development opportunities and invite colleagues from neighboring institutions to participate. Do what you can to enhance each other's missions. It is equally important to develop relationships in the community. Learn as much as possible about the people, and develop a foundation for future joint ventures. Be cautious about making promises to community groups, because you do not yet know if you will be able to deliver on them. Initial meetings should focus on relationship building and setting the stage for future opportunities to work together rather than accomplishing specific outcomes.

Critical Business Agenda

The new vice president should develop a critical business agenda—a list of high-priority items to be addressed in the near future. Frank discussion with the president and other members of the cabinet will be an important part of formulating this agenda. Consult closely with your management team, building on conversations and observations. Identify what is going well, where improvements can be made, and who will help implement changes. Incorporate performance expectations, benchmarks, standards, and other measures into the agenda. Align student affairs goals with institutional goals by referring to institutional documents such as the strategic plan, funding priorities, and annual reports. The effective vice president is the one who can connect student affairs to learning and the college to its students (Culp, 2011).

As the agenda takes form, you may be tempted to make changes quickly; however, it is wiser to wait and effect change slowly. Learn about the staff and use your experience and knowledge to mesh with institutional norms and values. Get to know the institution and the people. Gain additional insights into the culture and potential complicating factors. Capture the innocence of the honeymoon period while being receptive to concerns staff and others have about you as "the new person." A successful transition requires an inclusive approach to change over a reasonable period.

Identify areas for improvement and assign subcommittees to work on operational plans. Subcommittees should be staffed with high-potential individuals and subject matter experts—people who can formulate solutions to these concerns and drive improvement. Work with staff members on short- and long-term goals for the division. Keep the number of goals modest and include previously established institutional goals, where appropriate. Use these goals to start the change process and gradually establish a new direction for student affairs. Include a stretch goal or two to set the tone of high expectations, but make sure that most of the goals are realistic and achievable. Share your preliminary goals and invite feedback before they are finalized.

Meetings and Communication

Despite all the complaints about time wasted in team meetings, most people will admit that when they do not meet face-to-face (or at least electronically), communication breaks down. It is important, especially early in a new leader's tenure, to meet regularly. Stick to a tight agenda and meet for an hour or less. Staff members may offer recommendations on how to structure weekly meetings. Do not do all the talking yourself; share the stage with others. Meetings should be informative. If you just have update meetings, at which people talk about what they are working on, the staff will lose interest and consider the meetings a waste of time. Instead, include agenda items that have an impact on everyone and topics on which all members can have input.

Eventually, the new vice president should establish regular individual meetings with direct reports; this ensures that adequate time is spent with each one. Supervisor and employee must be able to count on quality time to discuss issues. Open door policies and "catch me when you need me" styles are fine, but dedicated, established times are important to ensure communication. The frequency of these meetings will vary depending on the experience of staff members, complexity of assignments, maturity of the staff, and many other factors. The meetings should be established and the frequency adjusted according to mutual expectations.

Lean toward overcommunication with and among your staff. Most problems result from a failure to communicate. Even as colleagues begin to get to know each other and each other's abilities, lack of clarity and incorrect assumptions may still occur. The vice president should use one-on-one meetings, full-staff meetings, e-mail, newsletters, and other devices to share information. Walking around and visiting with people is a good way to receive and provide information, but this method is ineffective for large numbers of people. Use a variety of methods and share information more than once.

Professional Development

The transition from one administration to another sometimes causes professional commitments to fall through the cracks. The new vice president should inquire about the division's professional memberships and professional development. Find out what the previous vice president subscribed to and belonged to, and determine what should be maintained, discontinued, or initiated. Find out which professional affiliations are preferred or possible. Regardless of institutional perspectives or policies, new vice presidents should at least maintain their individual professional memberships.

Professional development for new vice presidents is important and should not be ignored. The new role requires skills and knowledge not likely to have been obtained in previous positions. As professionals move from specialized management to higher level leadership positions, they need to be even more intentional about professional development. Some new vice presidents wish they had more knowledge about the various units for which they are responsible; for example, financial aid, enrollment management, accounting, and budgeting (Rodkin, 2011). Professional development resources can assist in this area, including the Institute for New Chief Student Affairs Officers, offered by the National Association of Student Personnel Administrators. Make a list of these resources and periodically review it.

The new vice president needs feedback to grow and develop, and observers are sure to have opinions about his or her actions during the transition. Solicit feedback from colleagues to gauge responses to your actions in the transition and adjust your style accordingly. Develop a thick skin and remain open to constructive criticism.

Routinely connect with institutional mentors and gather feedback from honest conversations. Strive to eliminate any gap between the president's expectations and your performance; determine the source of the disconnect and get connected again. Trusted internal mentors can provide perspective and uncover blind spots. If more than one person offers similar feedback, consider it to be valid and make appropriate adjustments.

Moving Forward

The honeymoon period is over. The new vice president is beginning to settle into a routine and stabilize the work setting. When this happens depends on direction provided by the president and the vice president's experience. At some point in the transition, you should be on your way to establishing the division's new culture. Focus on the continuing division work, strategic delivery of division services, efficient deployment of division resources, and continued division improvements. The lonely work of the transition period is coming to an end; turn your attention to working closely with the management team. In the end, the success of the new vice president for student affairs, management team, and the division are inextricably bound.

Continue to build on the relationships you established in the transition. Identifying and strengthening relationships with staff, colleagues, and influential people in the community can help direct your career and assist with work goals (RHR International, n.d.a). Whether you use these people as a sounding board, as resources for historical or political perspective, or just as trusted relationships, they are crucial to your long-term success. Seek guidance and wisdom from the president and others, but follow your instincts as you establish this inner circle of friends.

Meet with the president within the first 60 days to test potential structural changes in the division. This meeting is an important component as you set the course of change for the future. Your recommendations might include small, immediate adjustments as well as larger, dynamic shifts in the culture. Structural changes should be well thought out in terms of cost, short-term risk, and long-term benefit. Be sure the president understands and supports the recommended changes and suggested timeline. Depending on the scope of the structural changes and the campus culture, it might be prudent to also share these changes with the president's cabinet—at least in the form of an informational update.

Pitfalls to Avoid

Strong strategies, planning, and hard work will result in a successful executive transition. However, despite careful preparation and sound advice, new administrators sometimes sabotage their own efforts by not paying attention to potential pitfalls. Make sure you have good strategies in place to avoid these mistakes:

- Lack of a plan. Establish a plan for student affairs and provide direction. Following discussions with the president and other key stakeholders, plan the direction for the division and establish a few goals. Share them broadly and set the tone for reaching them.
- Vague expectations. Insist on receiving and giving clear directions regarding performance evaluation criteria. Spend time with the president to ensure that you know what is expected. Also, be crystal clear with others about your objectives for them. Let people know what is important.
- Not respecting the culture. Be aware of the local culture. Although change may be needed or expected, take care that it is implemented with dignity, respect for the past, and regard for local norms.
- Not setting the right tone in communications and appearance. Everything a new vice president says and does sets a tone and an example. Embrace this fact and use it as an advantage. Failure to do so will damage your momentum and credibility.
- Making changes too fast. The specific circumstances of the vice presidential turnover will determine the rate at which a new vice president can change the operation. Be careful not to change too many things or to change things too fast.

- Lack of a trusted institutional mentor. New vice presidents are hired because of their talents, skills, and experience. But all new executives can benefit from having an institutional mentor to share cultural information and practices. Failure to understand and incorporate this information can significantly limit the success of a new vice president.
- Not taking care of yourself. Any new job is stressful; if you are a top executive, the stress is intensified. Long hours, difficult situations, and few peers to consult with may wear you out. Make sure that you maintain your health, keep up with personal relationships, and pursue a balanced lifestyle.

Chapter Summary

Higher education—and student affairs in particular—is beginning to experience a shortage of qualified people who are interested in assuming the role of vice president. Many opportunities exist for those who are willing, but to be successful these professionals should prepare themselves and follow the advice of others.

Create a plan. Success is more likely to happen as the result of intentional actions. Before the first day, create a comprehensive plan; execute the plan for the first year to ensure acceptance, respect, and success. The new position and added responsibility will be a lot of work and will be stressful at times, but with a strong support system and a solid plan, you can enjoy your role: leading staff and serving students.

Prepare for the new role. To ensure long-term success, new vice presidents must do their homework before the first day of work. In preparing for the interview process, candidates should have done research into the institution's mission, values, vision, and operations.

Build relationships early. One of the most important tasks for a new employee is to develop professionally fulfilling, respectful, and caring relationships. These relationships take time to evolve, but they provide a strong foundation for future success. Begin on the first day by meeting people and learning about them. Connect to different groups on and off campus. Be intentional about building relationships with the president, direct reports, members of the division, and your peers.

What else

🛈 Learn about the institution and understand expectations. Determine what else is expected from the vice president for student affairs beyond what is listed on the organization chart. The president and others will have expectations, and you will be judged according to their performance measures. Understanding both the expectations and the performance measures will ensure that you pay attention to the right areas. You may be responsible for institutional data systems, student enrollment expectations, data about students, and state and federal guidelines. All these responsibilities might not be specifically mentioned; it is your responsibility to inquire.

🛈 Establish direction in the transition period. This involves: building a unified team that is committed to working together; developing a set of shared values; finding creative ways to partner with neighboring institutions and community members in joint opportunities; setting a critical business agenda for the highest priority items; developing a communication plan; making a commitment to personal and professional development; and focusing energy on moving forward. The support of institutional mentors cannot be overstated; new vice presidents should find both internal and external advisors who can provide honest feedback about their performance.

🛈 Avoid pitfalls. These strategies will be meaningless if you do not avoid common mistakes in executive transitions: lack of a plan, vague expectations, not respecting the culture, not setting the right tone, making changes too fast, lack of an institutional mentor, and not taking care of yourself. These are common errors that threaten even the most seasoned student affairs administrators.

References

Clement, L. M., & Rickard, S. T. (1992). *Effective leadership in student services: Voices from the field*. San Francisco, CA: Jossey-Bass.

Culp, M. M. (2011). Don't fence me in: The senior student affairs officer in the 21st-century community college. In G. J. Dungy & S. E. Ellis (Eds.), *Exceptional senior student affairs administrators' leadership: Strategies and competencies for success* (pp. 15–40). Washington, DC: National Association of Student Personnel Administrators.

Hewlett, S. A., Leader-Chivée, L., Sherbin, L., Gordon, J., & Dieudonné, F. (2012). *Executive presence*. New York, NY: Center for Talent Innovation.

Mead-Fox, D. (2009, April). Tackling the leadership scarcity. *The Chronicle of Higher Education*. Retrieved from http://chronicle.com/article/Tackling-the-Leadership/44809

MindTools. (n.d.). *Starting a new job: Getting used to your new role*. Retrieved from http://www.mindtools.com/pages/article/newCDV_29.htm

RHR International. (n.d.a). *Chief executive transitions: Keys to an effective transfer of leadership at the top*. Retrieved from http://www.rhrinternational.com/100127/pdf/rs/ChiefExecTransitions-Research-2012.pdf

RHR International. (n.d.b). Executive integration: Beyond the first 90 days. *Executive Insights, 23*(1). Retrieved from http://www.rhrinternational.com/100127/pdf/ei/V23N1-Executive-Integratio.pdf

Rodkin, D. M. (2011). *Leadership competencies of community college senior student affairs officers in the United States* (Doctoral dissertation). Retrieved from http://etd.fcla.edu/UF/UFE0043221/rodkin_d.pdf

CHAPTER 7

Assessing Campus and Divisional Cultures

W. Houston Dougharty and
JoNes R. VanHecke

While contemplating or actually making a professional transition, vice presidents for student affairs should return to activities that were informative in graduate school: investigating, assessing, and reflecting on the campus culture of a prospective or new campus, and assessing the division of student affairs. The authors review the importance and relevance of campus culture assessment activities and offer transitioning executives reminders and new ideas for effectively accomplishing such assessments of campuses and divisions. They provide insights from their own experience and that of vice presidential colleagues regarding both successful and problematic assessments during transitions into new senior student affairs positions.

Assessing campus cultures is an important and natural part of student affairs work. Many of us were drawn to student affairs, at least in part, because of our attraction to and affection for the college campus, the college experience, and the cultures and subcultures of the campus. Quite a few of our student affairs colleagues share our penchant for visiting campuses whenever we are in a new city, attracted by a highway sign that mentions a campus. We do this even while on vacation, oftentimes much to the annoyance of our families and traveling companions. However, this interest in campuses and their cultures can serve us exceedingly well as we contemplate and undertake an executive transition in student affairs—greatly informing us about ourselves and the various aspects of a campus culture that could predict a possible fit.

Most of us who did our graduate work (particularly master's degree) in a higher education student affairs program had courses and projects that placed a significant emphasis on assessing and understanding campus cultures. These days, it is rare to find a master's program that does not have a course called Campus Cultures or The College Campus. These courses include activities that formalize our natural desire to get to know what makes campuses tick, what makes them unique, and why folks are drawn to certain campus communities. These cultural investigations include reading related academic literature and campus documents of all sorts, becoming familiar with a variety of tools for assessing campus culture, visiting campuses and immersing oneself in their cultures, and reflecting on campus cultures and their implications for students and employees.

Campus Culture Assessment Literature

Although understanding campus culture is of critical importance to both the candidate and the newly hired vice president, many people find the idea of conducting such an assessment daunting. Existing literature about campus culture underscores the value of such efforts and provides insights into the benefits that can result from evaluating a campus and the culture of a student affairs division. The models and qualitative techniques described in this chapter provide frameworks that can help shape an approach to assessment.

Various authors offer nuanced definitions of *campus culture* (Cameron & Quinn, 2011) and *campus climate* (Hurtado, Milem, Clayton-Pedersen, & Allen, 1999; Rankin & Reason, 2008). We will not focus on subtle differences but, rather, note that both are ways to understand and make sense of a college community. The focus of this chapter is on how to assess campus climate and culture, ideally through a rigorous and encompassing examination of the campus experiences of faculty, staff, and students as expressed by attitudes, behaviors, traditions, and expectations. One effective approach is to ask how students, faculty, and staff experience the educational endeavor of a particular institution at a point in time.

Kezar and Eckel (2002) noted that "in the 1980s, organizational researchers from across various disciplines began examining the role of culture within organizational life. . . . Early research used culture to illustrate that campuses had unique cultures from other types of institutions, describing the myths and rituals of colleges, and student and faculty subculture" (p. 438). Subsequent studies linked culture with institutional functions such as governance (Chaffee & Tierney, 1988); leadership (Birnbaum, 1988); planning (Hearn, Clugston, & Heydinger, 1993; Leslie & Fretwell, 1996); and change (Curry, 1992; Guskin, 1996). Smart and St. John (1996) found that while organizational culture is often studied in higher education, "the linkages among different types of cultures, cultural strength, and organizational effectiveness have seldom been examined" (p. 220).

Creswell (1998) outlined several qualitative traditions that can provide a helpful lens through which to interpret campus culture: (1) biography and oral history (2) phenomenological study, and (3) ethnography. Biographies and oral histories use the study of an individual and his or her experience as an organizing framework. Biographies are challenging, because the researcher must "collect extensive information from and about the subject of the biography, . . . have a clear understanding of historical contextual material to position the subject within the larger trends in society or in the culture, and keep a keen eye to determine the particular stories, slant or angle" (Creswell, 1998, p. 51). Biographies and oral histories access specific and helpful information about a lived experience at a particular campus at a specific point in time, and thus provide a rich perspective from which to shape impressions of culture. Building on the biography, a phenomenological study seeks to understand the lived experiences of several individuals in a search for underlying meaning. Creswell (1998) noted that phenomenological study can be challenging because participants must be chosen carefully and many researchers find it difficult to bracket personal experiences. Finally, Creswell (1998) described ethnography as a "description or interpretation of a culture or social group or system [that] involves examining a group's observable and learned patterns of behavior, customs and way of life" (p. 58). Because successful ethnography entails prolonged observation in an immersion experience, this qualitative approach is not an option for an external candidate, but it could be an excellent approach for the newly hired vice president to adopt in the early weeks and months of the job.

Culture and Climate Assessment Models

Numerous models exist that can help frame campus culture assessment. This section highlights three models and offers a few data indicators and key questions the transitioning vice president for student affairs might find helpful. These indicators and questions are not intended to be comprehensive; rather, they suggest possibilities to consider. Savvy candidates and newly hired vice presidents can use the models to help organize their campus culture explorations.

Rankin and Reason Model

Rankin and Reason (2008) suggested a five-phase model to help campuses understand the challenges they are facing (see Table 7.1). "Five areas within the higher education system that influence campus climate are identified in the model: (1) access/retention, (2) research/scholarship, (3) inter- and intragroup relations, (4) curriculum and pedagogy, and (5) university policy and service. A sixth area, external relations, was added to the model in 2006 based on the results of recent assessments" (p. 266).

Table 7.1
Rankin and Reason Model

Areas That Influence Campus Climate	Data Indicators and Questions to Explore
Access/retention	• Demographics for all aspects of the enrollment process (inquiry, application, acceptance, and matriculation) • Retention rates for various groups • Retention efforts (Who is responsible for retention? Who is engaged in the work?)
Research/scholarship	• Do institutional policies support diverse perspectives and methodologies? • Are policies and practices around research and scholarship institutionalized?
Inter- and intragroup relations	• Does programming support intergroup interactions? • Are there functioning student groups organized around identities?
Curriculum and pedagogy	• Is the curriculum designed to support campus values? • What resources are available for faculty to improve the teaching-learning environment?
University policy and service	• What policies convey commitment to institutional values? • How easy or difficult is it to implement changes in policies and services?
External relations	• What role do external constituencies play in shaping campus culture? • Which campus stakeholders identify external relations as an area of key concern?

Cameron and Quinn Model

Cameron and Quinn (2011) offered another helpful model for understanding campus climate (see Table 7.2). Their Organizational Culture Assessment Instrument diagnoses organizational culture via six dimensions (dominant characteristics, organizational leadership, management of employees, organizational glue, strategic emphases, and criteria for success). The dimensions are based on the Competing Values Framework, a theoretical framework of how organizations work and the values on which they are founded. The framework is divided into four quadrants (collaborate, create, compete, and control)—each quadrant represents a way of being, seeing, managing, and organizing. This model provides specific questions for campus culture assessment and is easily searchable on the Internet.

Table 7.2
Cameron and Quinn Model

Dimensions of Organizational Culture	Data Indicators and Questions to Explore
Dominant characteristics	• Is the place personal? Do people share information about themselves? • Are people willing to take risks? • Are people competitive or collaborative? • Do formal procedures govern what people do, or do people determine what is best?
Organizational leadership	• Do leaders mentor and facilitate? • Are leaders risk takers? • Are leaders results oriented? • Are leaders organized and efficient?

Management of employees	• Are teamwork and collaboration emphasized? • Are innovation and uniqueness valued? • Are employees expected to produce results and achieve? • Does the organization value secure employment and stable relationships?
Organizational glue	• Does commitment to the place run high? • How important is it to be on the cutting edge? • What happens when goals are not met? • Is it difficult to introduce change? How often are processes reviewed and altered?
Strategic emphases	• Are trust, openness, and participation valued? • Are new ways of thinking encouraged? • Are targets set and met? Are stretch goals used? If so, how public are they? • How much importance is given to smooth operations?
Criteria for success	• Is success based on concern for people? • How important are new products in judging success? • What benchmarks are used to determine success in the marketplace? • Are resources allocated on the basis of judgments of success?

Note. Table adapted from Cameron and Quinn (2011), Figure 2.1 The Organizational Culture Assessment Instrument–Current Profile, pp. 30–32.

Hurtado, Milem, Clayton-Pedersen, and Allen Model

College campus climate often refers to how individuals and groups experience membership in the campus community and the quality and extent of interaction among various groups and individuals. Using this context, Hurtado, Milem, Clayton-Pedersen, and Allen (1999) offered a four-dimensional framework that is helpful for holistic understanding (see Table 7.3). Their model proposes that campus climate can be studied using four dimensions: historical context of exclusion or inclusion, structural or compositional dimension, psychological dimension, and behavioral dimension.

Table 7.3

Hurtado, Milem, Clayton-Pedersen, and Allen Model

Dimensions of Campus Climate	Data Indicators and Questions to Explore
Historical context of exclusion/inclusion	• Policy shifts • Campus protests • Lawsuits • Changes in legal interpretations
Structural or compositional	• Salary and benefits equitability • Numbers of minorities, women, and lesbian, gay, bisexual, and transgender (LGBT) students, faculty, and staff • Percentages of minorities, women, and LGBT students, faculty, and staff • Numbers and percentages in various disciplines, majors, and senior leadership positions
Psychological	• Perception of belonging • Perception of alienation • Perception of conflict
Behavioral	• Experience with mainstream campus experiences • Interactions among various groups

Note. Table adapted from Williams (2010), Figure 2.1 Four Dimensions of the Higher Education Campus Climate, p.10.

Models such as these three can provide helpful organizational strategies for assessing the culture and campus climate of an institution. The clearest understanding of a place is often from the inside, so use these and similar frameworks to develop questions to ask insiders during telephone, offsite, and onsite interviews, or in initial meetings.

The techniques and models described provide frameworks that can help both the candidate and the newly hired vice president to assess campus culture. However, most people will employ multiple strategies to accomplish this important task. We discuss a few of these strategies below.

Culture Assessment Strategies From a Distance

Compared to previous generations, today's vice presidential colleagues can more easily investigate campus cultures from afar thanks to the advent of technology and the Internet. While we will discuss the ever-valuable strategies of networking and using firsthand resources, most will probably conduct an Internet search on campuses before doing anything else. The convenience and power of the Internet enable us to gain access to large amounts of helpful information at the click of a mouse or touch of a tablet device.

The Internet

For those who have been in the field for more than a couple decades, the Internet is a tool that was not available when we were learning the ropes of campus culture assessment in graduate school. (Those who have gone to graduate school recently probably cannot even imagine that pre-Internet reality.) Today, the Internet offers a wealth of information, and we must be diligent in determining which sources are the most trustworthy. Without leaving our desks, couches, or deck chairs, we can visit campuses virtually in ways that expose us to a wide range of facts, observations, opinions, and images that can inform our culture assessment.

A terrific place to start is the college or university website itself. It holds a trove of information that is both highly edited and shaped by campus leadership, as well as pages deeper in the website that invite us to view the campus from a variety of formal and quite informal perspectives. The institution's .edu site is a perfect launching pad. Sarah Westfall, vice president for student development and dean of students at Kalamazoo College, noted that she advises vice presidential colleagues to "learn what you can from the documentary information, typically on the website; pay attention to the recent history of the place, read public addresses by the president, find out who the trustees are, read the mission statement, read the human resources information, and swim around the site" (personal communication, January 28, 2013).

Certain sections of a campus website can be particularly helpful for establishing context and getting a feel for the campus. Sections related to campus history, mission and vision, values, strategic plans, and learning outcomes provide newcomers with answers to questions related to inter- and intragroup relations (Rankin and Reason Model), organizational glue (Cameron and Quinn Model), and historical context (Hurtado, Milem, Clayton-Pedersen, and Allen Model). Sections on the website related to administrative leadership structure, board of trustees/regents, organizational charts, and campus governance are ideally suited for informing candidates and newcomers about organizational leadership (Cameron and Quinn Model). In an effort to be thorough, candidates should also study sections on the website related to institutional research data, recent press releases, campus calendars, admissions information, alumni and community relations, and parent information.

Institutional Research

Institutional research is a particularly important section to explore, given the fact that data inform so many decisions at the senior level. Peg Blake from Humboldt State University shared that she considers looking at data resources as an imperative. "I always scour a university's webpages for data—usually found in the institutional research operation—to learn as much as I can about the institution. Reading annual reports, understanding enrollment trends, and learning about student engagement efforts are good ways to understand the life of the university" (P. Blake, personal communication, January 21, 2013).

Student Affairs Websites

One section of the campus website that deserves attention is the student affairs division. Sometimes a divisional site can be difficult to find or may not exist—which in itself is telling. Once on a student affairs, student services, or vice president for student affairs/dean of students page, certain areas can inform a culture assessment.

Important information about the division's focus can be found in the text of the mission, vision, value, learning outcomes, and student affairs committee structures. Sections on staffing, departments, programs, facilities related to student affairs, and emergency procedures can say a lot about the scope of the division and campuswide expectations. Information related to the student handbook, student government, and student organizations can hold important clues about the role students play in advancing the division.

Some small college student affairs divisions might not have a strong web presence, or the web presence might be diffuse or disjointed. This is not a reason to lose interest in a senior executive position, nor should it deter prospective candidates from seeking information from other sources. In fact, this deficiency is a viable growth opportunity for the incoming vice president.

Third Party Websites

Much can be learned from third parties that have insights and opinions about the campus and its virtues and weaknesses. Recent years have seen a proliferation of college and university guides and lists—some more legitimate and data-driven than others. Many of these lists rely on subjective appraisals by students, alumni, and employees, including quotes and open blogs. Be aware of the sources of the information in these guides and lists, as well as the possible editorial slant of the publisher. The following are some popular sites:

- *U.S. News and World Report* (www.usnews.com/education)
- Big Future by the College Board (https://bigfuture.collegeboard.org)
- Peterson's (www.petersons.com)
- The Princeton Review (www.princetonreview.com)
- Zinch (www.zinch.com)
- *The Huffington Post* (www.huffingtonpost.com/news/college-rankings)
- College Confidential (www.collegeconfidential.com)
- Cappex (www.cappex.com)
- College Suggest (www.collegesuggest.com)
- College Prowler (http://collegeprowler.com)

Other third party sources on the Internet are sponsored by organizations in the community where the campus is located. Some of these websites might be linked to the campus website—on the admissions, community relations, or parent relations pages—but you will find most of them by searching for the state/province, city, town, or neighborhood. Helpful community-based sites include the following:

- Chambers of commerce
- City/town governments
- School systems
- Arts programs
- Local public transportation agencies
- Health facilities
- Parks and recreation
- Local newspapers and media outlets
- Cost-of-living calculators

You can also "like" the Facebook page of a college or division, or follow campus Twitter accounts. By the time this book is printed, there will likely be a dozen additional ways to tap into the culture of a campus electronically.

The upside for the vice president for student affairs in transition is that this wealth of information is right at our fingertips. Online content must be read and analyzed in a discerning and critical fashion, with awareness of and sensitivity to the inherent biases of the many authors who create these websites.

Networks and Firsthand Experiences

Using the Internet is a quick and inexpensive way to get a lot of information about a campus, but more traditional networks and firsthand strategies have their place. The assessment will be fuller and more informative if it includes insights from individual perspectives, whether gathered from colleagues and other networks or from people directly connected to the institution (firsthand sources). Henry Toutain, vice president for student affairs at Kenyon College, shared his reflections on his multiple transitions to vice presidential positions:

> I gathered a good deal of valuable information—especially concerning campus culture, community values, and operational realities—"on the ground" from professional colleagues with both (1) an understanding of the scope, demands, and opportunities of a vice president for student affairs position, and (2) extensive knowledge of the prospective institution. Of course, what must also be assessed, and critically so, is the extent, sophistication, and perspectives on the profession of one's colleagues, as well as the depth, breadth, and balance of their understanding and views of the institution. (personal communication, February 12, 2013)

In other words, whom you ask for input can be as important as what you learn from them. Try to identify voices from a wide array of perspectives, then listen for the similarities and differences in what they say.

In assessing an institution's culture or climate, it is important to remember that individuals interpret the behavior and language of others through their own cultural biases and that each person's beliefs, values, and assumptions become their own reality. As a new vice president, you will have to determine whether a particular person's lived experience represents the whole community.

Anonymous Sources

One of the challenges of using firsthand strategies during an executive transition is the desire or need for anonymity and confidentiality. Often aspiring vice presidents must be discreet about their searches for information, both to protect their current position and to carefully and wisely apply for another position. An effective first step is to identify trusted colleagues and friends who are familiar with the prospective campus, its division of student affairs, or the location. Confidential informational interviews with trusted informants can be very helpful in contextualizing the information you have gained electronically. An added benefit is that the colleague or friend knows you and is likely to have an opinion about how you would fit in at the other campus.

Prospective Peers

A second critical group from whom to gather information is your prospective supervisor and peers, cabinet-level colleagues, and the president. Most interview processes build in time for the candidate to meet with the president and other vice presidents. Make the most of these opportunities by being prepared with questions (e.g., those provided earlier with the three models) that will help you understand the campus dynamics. Come prepared to respectfully pose challenging questions. Westfall suggested:

> [W]hen interviewing with the president, ask what they envision for the role and, specifically, about things they hope to change institutionally and in the division. When interviewing with other cabinet-level folks, ask what it's like to work with/ for the president. Ask what cabinet meetings are like, and how disagreements play out. . . . It's also important to get a feel, if possible, about any distance between colleagues inherited by the president and those hired by the president. (personal communication, January 28, 2013)

Follow up on these individual conversations via phone or e-mail to clarify your impressions. Sometimes people are reluctant to speak openly in group interview sessions but will share more frankly in a one-on-one conversation.

Search Consultants

Campuses often use search consultants to fill positions at the executive level. These "head hunters" can be excellent resources for assessing the culture of a campus and its environs. Often consultants are happy to research a particular area of interest for a candidate, ranging from information about the history and current condition of the division to the quality and availability of local schools for your children. Frank conversations with a search consultant can be helpful to clarify confusing or contradictory material you have gathered over the course of your assessment process. Remember, though, that the consultant is working for the campus and is charged with identifying and delivering qualified candidates.

People Your Colleagues Know

While you may not have direct contacts, ask colleagues to identify people they know who are currently working at the institution you are considering. This strategy can be effective when you are seeking input from outside student affairs and especially from faculty members. Asking trusted faculty friends and colleagues if they have contacts at the new institution can lead you to information not typically available in the context of the search process and to insights from different perspectives about the position and the student affairs division.

Mentors and Trusted Colleagues

In addition to talking with people who know the institution you are considering, Toutain said he has found special value in the "opinions and perspectives of longstanding professional colleagues and mentors who understood *me*, my strengths/weaknesses, and my personal and professional values, and who were willing to share their candid observations of how well these things aligned" (personal communication, February 12, 2013). Mentors, partners, and friends who know you should not be overlooked as helpful sounding boards. Toutain said, "In spite of my having pored over documents and web content, and spoken with individuals who had considerable history and deep understanding of the places for my potential relocation, some very interesting and sometimes surprising observations and questions invariably emerged from this discernment exercise" (personal communication, February 12, 2013).

Campus Visit

As we often tell students, there is no substitute for actually spending time on the campus to get a genuine feel for the culture of the place. It may be hard to remain incognito if you are a known candidate, but you might be able to slip into campus events, tag along on a campus tour, or simply use a map to take yourself on a tour of the campus, visiting venues that will help you pick up the campus vibe—for example, the student center, museums or galleries, athletics facilities, classroom buildings, administrative offices, neighborhood shops and restaurants, and the library. Determine what is important to the college community by observing where it invests its resources and how the campus is maintained.

Picking up "artifacts" (e.g., posters, flyers, brochures, magazines, or newspapers) during the visit can be quite informative. Look for visual representations of the college's mission and goals. Note whether the institution communicates its values to the community. For example, Gustavus Adolphus College uses visually attractive words and photographs to illustrate the institution's five core values on the five pillars in the campus dining center. Integrating your personal observations with all the other data and impressions you have collected can provide a great deal of insight about the fit between you and the potential employer.

Confirming Your Impressions

During the on-campus interview process, remember that transitions between interview sessions, free time, and mealtimes are opportunities for you to test your impressions and double check what you have heard in more casual environments. Conversations with students are less structured and, when appropriate, can provide opportunities for you to learn about significant campus issues from the student perspective. Remember, in addition to being interviewed, you are interviewing the campus.

The First 6 Weeks

Finally, do not underestimate the power of your first few weeks as the new vice president for student affairs. Viewing the first 6 weeks as a valuable time for learning about the culture of your new campus can mean a smooth and ultimately successful transition. As Westfall noted:

> [O]nce in the new job (or beforehand, in my case), meet individually with each direct report and ask some general questions: What should I know about you? About your role in the division? About the division? What do you like about working here? What would you change? This helped me gather a lot of information very early on that "held" over time. It helped me gauge who the high-maintenance folks were, and gave me a sense of how they viewed themselves as a broad unit. (personal communication, January 28, 2013)

Such efforts signal to your new colleagues that you are interested in knowing them and in understanding the campus culture.

Hits, Misses, and Musts

Executives who have navigated a transition to vice president for student affairs have used (with varying degrees of success) many of the distance and firsthand strategies and resources described above. The authors, and a number of our colleagues, have reflected on our experiences conducting assessments of campus cultures, divisions, and locations while considering an executive transition and want to share some of our successes, failures, and insights in three appropriately named categories: Hits, Misses, and Musts.

Hits are the strategies that worked well for us and played a significant role in our ability to understand and navigate a campus culture. *Misses* are attempts we made that either did not turn out to be helpful or perhaps even backfired. *Musts* are the nuggets of culture assessment advice we would recommend to everyone who is investigating a campus culture or subcultures in preparation for embarking on an executive transition. The advice offered below comes from sitting vice presidents and deans of students affairs (including the authors) at diverse institutions throughout the United States.

Hits

Following are a few campus culture assessments that paid off.

- A vice president for student affairs who is just seven months into his new position suggests a thought process that worked well for him as he learned about and visited campuses: *I used a deductive reasoning process in order to learn as much as possible about my new campus's culture. The framework I used included asking myself the following questions as I encountered various aspects of the campus: What do I understand about the institution—its history, culture, values, idiosyncrasies and broken records; short- and long-term hopes and dreams; and the campus political climate?*

- Here's another successful strategy he used when visiting the campus and after arriving there to start in his position: *I tried to meet and get to know students in the places where they chose to be. Where are these places? What is it that they like to do? I put myself "in the mix"—trying to tap into their issues and interests, both significant and seemingly mundane. Some told me exactly what I knew or believed to be true, while others surprised me and provided me with the gift of unexpected possibilities.*

- One vice president who has experienced three executive transitions likes to be an early bird for on-campus interviews: *Whenever possible, I like to see the campus before even applying—to have an incognito visit in jeans and a sweatshirt, bopping around campus as if I am a prospective parent or donor. I particularly like to hang out in the campus center and the coffee shops, walk through the library and the academic buildings, the administrative offices. I listen and look at every turn, trying to pick up the vibe of the place. Reading bulletin boards and picking up student, town, and campus publications. Before an actual campus interview, I try to negotiate an arrival the day before my schedule begins and scout out all the locations I'll be visiting during the interview—it calms my nerves and provides a sense of familiarity. If I run into people I recognize or know, I say hello and express my enthusiasm for being on campus. It also provides me with a sense of what's happening on campus now. Of course, discretion is important, as another candidate might be interviewing that day.*

- A veteran vice president for student affairs recalls a strategy he used within the division after arriving on a new campus to start his job: *When I arrived, the student affairs division was focusing on providing quality programs and services. However, I knew the president selected me because of my emphasis on and experience in the learning aspect of student affairs work and my desire to connect more closely with academic affairs. While some staff did not take to this new direction and resisted, others seemed hungry for a new approach and jumped in with both feet. I made sure to engage these staff members in prominent leadership roles in the development of our divisional learning outcomes, and their involvement had a very positive ripple effect on the rest of the division staff.*

- Another vice president who is nearly a decade into a first executive position recalls the importance of connections through professional organizations: *Talking with friends in my professional organizations who had history with or knowledge about the campus was critical. They provided me with information and insights that were particularly valuable. After I moved into the position, I got immediately involved in the state student affairs organization and the regional NASPA (National Association of Student Personnel Administrators) community—particularly connecting with other vice presidents for student affairs, both veteran and new. I recommend using these networks within the professional organizations intentionally and often.*

Misses

Some vice presidents' efforts to size up a campus culture did not turn out the way they planned.

- A first-time vice president wishes he had spent more time thinking about the culture beyond the student affairs division itself: *My assessment of student life centered mostly on the staff in the division and did not extend far enough beyond the staff and the programs I would be leading. As I think back, I missed a lot of cues about how the rest of the campus perceives student life. If I could go back to my first weeks on campus, I would conduct a listening tour with other areas, including both administrative and academic folks, as well as a wide range of student and alumni groups.*

- One veteran vice president for student affairs misread the quality of the president's relationship with the faculty: *During the search process, I naively assumed that the president for whom I would be working had a very positive and collegial relationship with the faculty. I based this assumption primarily on the interactions I had with faculty during my airport and campus interviews. What I did not consider is that often the faculty on the search committee and those who meet with candidates are a select bunch who are likely to be supporters of the president. Had I scratched a little deeper—like reaching out to faculty who were not on my schedule or asking faculty friends on my current campus if they knew faculty on my prospective campus I could talk to—it would have been clear that there was friction and even animus. While I may not have made a different decision, I would have at least had my eyes wide open to the possibility that some (very vocal!) faculty would be suspicious of anyone this president hired.*

- A first-time vice president wishes she had more thoroughly investigated the board of trustees: *I wish I had asked more about the expectations and norms related to interacting with trustees. While all my surprises have been happy ones, were I to do it again I would focus more carefully on this key constituency during the process.*

- Another vice president describes a regrettable miscalculation: *The search committee for the new vice president for student affairs included a senior academic leader who had been a vocal critic of the previous student affairs culture. In fact, I believe she was on the search committee because of her outspoken remarks about the need for a new direction. After accepting the position, I connected with this senior leader because it was important to me to get connected with academic leadership and faculty, and I wanted to get this person's guidance on how best to do so. I subsequently followed her suggestions carefully, in some cases setting aside my own ideas, in an effort to gain favor with this highly respected student affairs critic. However, I later discovered that, while this person was indeed respected by faculty and other academic administrators, her perspectives on student-affairs-related matters were not universally shared. My efforts to win over one prominent critic led me to focus my assessment of the academic culture too narrowly and, thus, miss early opportunities to connect and engage with other faculty and the broader academic community.*

- A first-time vice president believes that more knowledge about campus unions would have helped in understanding and navigating the culture: *I completely underestimated the influence of bargaining unit/union culture in my first transition as a vice president for student affairs. I naively thought that my lack of experience with bargaining unit culture would be surmounted by my approach: building relationships and facilitating conversations. My approach had limited success, as I*

141

experienced that the conversation in union culture occurred in silos, and not across bargaining units. In the end, the knowledge of that reality has played a significant factor in thinking about pursuing a new position.

Musts

In order to make a successful culture assessment during an executive transition, consider the following:

- Pay attention to the language and themes in the position description and to the language used by and observations of the search consultant. What strikes you or stands out in any way? Do certain word choices seem to have special currency or weight? Does the description sound as though it is talking about you?

- Whom are you replacing if you take this position? What are (or were) the circumstances of this person's departure? Find out as much as you can about the predecessor or incumbent. The person's accomplishments are important to understand, as are his or her reasons for leaving. Pay close attention to what others say about that person—before and during the search and transition processes.

- Trust your gut. You have succeeded in student affairs because you have good judgment and are sensitive to important signals that others send you. While the culture assessment process needs to be thoughtful, intelligent, and deliberative, you should not ignore how you are feeling or the messages your instincts are sending you. If something seems too good to be true, it probably is not completely true.

- Be bold about asking any questions that might be nagging at you as you learn more about the campus. It is always better to know where the bodies are buried and the landmines located. You might ask "What are senior leadership meetings like?" or "When there is a crisis, how do people typically respond to each other?" or "How do faculty perceive, understand, and value our work in student affairs?" or "How do disagreements typically play out here?"

- Find out where folks at the institution come from, in the student affairs division and beyond. What is the mix from outside and within the campus? In the division, what is the level of professional preparation? Academic catalogs are excellent resources for this information.

- Learn as much as you can about the president—the importance of this relationship cannot be underestimated. What is the president's history and background? What did he or she accomplish (or not) in previous positions and institutions? Ask other senior staff who work or have worked for him or her about the president's style, demeanor, and vision. In fact, ask many of these same questions of the president, too.

- Be observant on campus. Are people smiling? Do folks interact with each other? What nonverbal messages do you get during conversations? Pay close attention to posters and signs, the condition of the buildings and grounds, the quality of the publications, and the general feel of the campus and the people there.

As student affairs educators, we are often the first to suggest that much learning can come from doing, but we can also learn a great deal if we pay attention to what those who have gone before us have done. Take advantage of the stories and experiences of vice presidents for student affairs who have researched and explored campus cultures and navigated executive transitions. Doing so will help you add to your own lists of hits and musts and avoid the misses.

Finding a Cultural Fit

Student affairs professionals are, by the very nature of our work, campus ethnographers. We are naturally drawn to campuses and should fully and intentionally exploit that tendency. It is important for senior student affairs officials who are considering or in the midst of an executive transition to employ strategies—both old and new—to thoroughly investigate, assess, and reflect on the new campus culture. Vice presidents will benefit from using proven methods to effectively assess the campus and the division, and from embracing the insights of vice presidential colleagues regarding both successful and problematic assessments they have made in their own transitions.

By familiarizing yourself with the literature of campus culture assessment and using multiple distance and firsthand assessment strategies, you can determine the likelihood of a good fit with the new campus before you make a significant commitment to the application or employment process. Newly hired vice presidents for student affairs can also benefit from the use of campus culture assessment strategies that, when applied thoroughly, are likely to lead to smoother transitions. The more thorough and discerning the culture assessment, the greater the potential for a successful match between the new vice president for student affairs and the campus.

Chapter Summary

Assessing campus cultures is an important and natural part of student affairs work. This interest in campuses and their cultures can be exceedingly helpful as you contemplate and undertake an executive transition—providing insights into the various aspects of a campus culture that could predict a possible fit at a new institution. This chapter focused on how to assess campus climate and culture through a broad and rigorous examination of the experiences of faculty, staff, and students as expressed by attitudes, behaviors, traditions, and expectations.

⊕ Academic literature is a good place to start. Organizational researchers from various disciplines have examined the role of culture in organizational life. Early research on institutions of higher education demonstrated that campus cultures were different from those of other types of institutions. Researchers described the myths and rituals of colleges, and student and faculty subcultures.

- Other methods for interpreting campus include biographies and oral histories, and phenomenological and ethnographic studies.

- Three culture and climate assessment models are discussed. You can use any of them to help organize your campus culture explorations. Each model includes data indicators and key questions to ask.

- Distance strategies to assist in your exploration include: searching the Internet; following the institution's social media channels; and exploring the institution's website (particularly the institutional research page and student affairs section) as well as third party websites (e.g., college and university guides, chambers of commerce, city governments, school systems).

- Networks and firsthand experiences provide individual perspectives from current and prospective colleagues, friends, friends of friends, and mentors. A campus visit can be very enlightening, and your own observations in the first 6 weeks are crucial to complete the picture.

- Executives who have navigated a transition to vice president offer a list of hits, misses, and musts in the use of these strategies. Hits are the strategies that worked well and played a significant role in helping the person understand the new campus culture. Misses did not help—some even backfired. Musts are nuggets of culture assessment advice the authors would recommend to everyone who is investigating a campus culture in preparation for an executive transition.

References

Birnbaum, R. (1988). *How college works.* San Francisco, CA: Jossey-Bass.

Cameron, K. S., & Quinn, R. E. (2011). *Diagnosing and changing organizational culture: Based on the Competing Values Framework* (3rd ed.). San Francisco, CA: Jossey-Bass.

Chaffee, E. & Tierney, W. (1988). *Collegiate culture and leadership strategies.* New York, NY: American Council on Education and Macmillan.

Creswell, J. W. (1998). *Qualitative inquiry and research design: Choosing among five traditions.* Thousand Oaks, CA: Sage.

Curry, B. K. (1992). *Instituting enduring innovations: Achieving continuity of change in higher education* (ASHE-ERIC Higher Education Vol. 21, No. 7). Washington, DC: The George Washington University.

Guskin, A. E. (1996). Facing the future: The change process in restructuring universities. *Change, 28*(4), 27–37.

Hearn, J. C., Clugston, R., & Heydinger, R. (1993). Five years of strategic environmental assessment at a research university: A case study of an organizational innovation. *Innovative Higher Education, 18*(1), 7–36.

Hurtado, S., Milem, J., Clayton-Pedersen, A., & Allen, W. (1999). *Enacting diverse learning environments: Improving the climate for racial/ethnic diversity in higher education* (ASHE-ERIC Higher Education Report Vol. 26, No. 8). Washington, DC: The George Washington University.

Kezar, A., & Eckel, P. (2002). The effect of institutional culture on change strategies in higher education: Universal principles or culturally responsive concepts? *Journal of Higher Education, 73*(4), 435–460.

Leslie, D., & Fretwell, L. (1996). *Wise moves in hard times.* San Francisco, CA: Jossey-Bass.

Magolda, P. M. (1999). Using ethnographic fieldwork and case studies to guide student affairs practice. *Journal of College Student Development, 40*(1), 10–21.

Magolda, P. M. (2001). What our rituals tell us about community on campus. *About Campus, 5*(2), 2–8.

Rankin, S. R., & Reason, R. D. (2008). Transformational tapestry model: A comprehensive approach to transforming campus climate. *Journal of Diversity in Higher Education, 1*(4), 262–274.

Smart, J. C., & St. John, E. P. (1996). Organizational culture and effectiveness in higher education: A test of the culture type and strong culture hypotheses. *Educational Evaluation and Policy Analysis, 16*(3), 219–241.

Williams, D.A. (2010). *Florida Gulf Coast University campus climate study: Taking strides towards a better future, final report, April 2010.* Retrieved on June 16, 2013 from www.fgcu.edu/president/files/FGCU_Climate_Culture_Report_2010.pdf

PART II

Transition Stories

Bait and Switch *double check position description*

Ainsley Carry, Arthur Sandeen, and Brandi Hephner LaBanc

Andy Carr was selected as the new vice president for student affairs at Northern University. Carr looked forward to leading a comprehensive division of student affairs at which he would be responsible for orchestrating an array of departments to serve students' needs. However, in his first 2 weeks on the job he made a disappointing discovery: The position description was grossly inaccurate.

Institutional Background

Northern University is a 150-year-old land grant, sea grant, and space grant institution in the northeastern United States. The school boasts more than 140 academic degree programs, 12 academic colleges, three professional schools, and first-class research facilities. The campus is 51 percent women and 49 percent men, with less than 10 percent minority students. Northern University has a long history of governance battles. Throughout the institution's history, various groups—trustees, faculty, students, and staff—have engaged in power struggles. In the 1980s and 1990s, the board of trustees micromanaged the university to the point of making personnel decisions. Board members regularly involved themselves in personnel decisions regarding faculty, staff, and athletic coaches. They inserted themselves into student enrollment and student housing decisions. It was not unusual for a board member to advocate publicly for the termination of a faculty member or to meet with an academic dean to criticize how a particular curriculum was structured. Faculty governance groups struggled for recognition and respect during the years when the board of trustees was operating beyond its boundaries, and clashes between the two groups were documented in the media. Student governance has seen an equal amount of volatility over the years. Alumni from the 1970s and 1980s brag about how much power student government and Greek letter organizations used to have in making decisions about student life. The administration was very hands-off with students in those decades, but it toughened up as threats of litigation increased after student deaths and serious injuries. In the early 2000s, faculty governance reemerged after a series of trustee decisions attracted negative attention to the university.

Division of Student Affairs Background

The Division of Student Affairs has evolved over several decades. In the early 1960s, 1970s, and 1980s, student life was shaped by a strong Greek system that assumed most of the responsibility for creating outside-the-classroom experiences for students. In that era, the dean of men and dean of women were among the highest level administrators; they focused on mentorship and discipline. In the 1980s, when the dean of women retired, the Division of Student Affairs moved to a single dean of students. Jim Roy was appointed the first dean of students. The portfolio evolved over the years, until the position had responsibility for almost everything outside the classroom: housing and residence life; learning communities; campus recreation; enrollment management (admissions, financial aid, registrar); the student center; student activities; the community service office; testing services; services for students with disabilities; student conduct; academic advising; new student orientation; the career center; dining services; campus safety services; the bookstore; the student infirmary; student counseling services; and student leadership programs. As the profession evolved, the institution adopted new student programs and services, which were housed in student affairs. From the 1950s to the mid-1990s, the Division of Student Affairs doubled in personnel, scope, and responsibility. In 1995, Roy retired after 40 years as a dean.

With advice from hiring consultants and accreditation agencies, Northern University reviewed the Division of Student Affairs to determine the best method to move forward with replacing Dean Roy. A small group of faculty members thought this would be a good time to break up the massive division, because they believed that the student voice in governance issues was overwhelming the faculty perspective. The chair of the faculty senate suggested that much of the Division of Student Affairs should be outsourced and the remaining departments should move under academic affairs. The accreditation agency and consultants disagreed; instead, they recommended that the position of dean of students be upgraded to vice president and that the university hire a professional who could mend relationships with faculty groups yet keep students engaged in institutional decision making. In 1995, Northern University hired its first vice president for student affairs. Consultants agreed that the scope of the portfolio and expectations for budgetary responsibilities required the skills of a seasoned professional at the vice presidential level. They hoped to attract high-caliber candidates by upgrading the title and salary to match the demands of the position.

The university conducted a national search. The successful candidate was Walter Wright, who had more than 20 years of experience in college administration; he completed his education in the south and had spent his entire career so far working at southern institutions. His welcome at Northern University was warm, but his tenure was short-lived—his values clashed with the traditions and practices of students and board members at Northern University. In his first 12 months, Wright battled against long-standing student traditions he viewed as dangerous and discriminating to some student populations. He battled against the Greek system, which had a stranglehold on key student leadership positions and which marginalized women and minority groups. He cracked down on organizational rituals that were now considered hazing. He did not have time to develop faculty relationships and connect with members of the board of trustees. After 5 years, complaints from students and staff members to board members and the president's office were too numerous to be ignored. No one—student, faculty, staff member, or board member—was willing to speak in Wright's defense. As a result, he was given the choice of accepting another position at the university or being fired. He elected to accept another position at the university.

In preparing to advertise the vice president for student affairs position again after 5 years, members of the faculty senate approached the president and again requested that much of the division be outsourced or dismantled, and the leadership position returned to a dean of students position. Because he had ignored them 5 years earlier, the president felt pressure to listen to the faculty this time. He moved some departments to academic affairs: enrollment management, testing services, career center, counseling services, student infirmary, learning communities, academic advising, and services for students with disabilities. He relocated dining services, housing and residence life, campus safety, and the bookstore to auxiliary services. The previously robust division now included only the student center, student activities, campus recreation, student leadership programs, and the community service office. Rather than hiring a new vice president for student affairs, the president appointed a faculty member as interim dean of students until a more permanent solution was devised.

Five years later, Northern University hired a new president. President John Grant began his administration by conducting listening tours with key constituent groups: students, faculty, staff, board members, and parents. The experiment that involved redistributing departments from the Division of Student Affairs and appointing a faculty member to serve as interim dean of students received mixed reviews; faculty were satisfied with the new authority over areas in which they previously had no decision-making power, but students felt as if their voice and influence had been eliminated. Even the board of trustees commented on the need to rebuild the division and hire a professionally trained vice president for student affairs. Grant had served at other institutions where the role of the vice president for student affairs was valued; he followed the advice of students and the board. In his second year, he initiated a national search for a new vice president for student affairs.

Andy Carr's Background

Andy Carr completed his education at an institution in the North and had more than 20 years of college administrative experience at five institutions of higher education across the country. He was a sitting vice president at a large state institution with favorable marks from students, faculty, and staff. Carr taught in the higher education administration program; however, more than 90 percent of his time was devoted to administrative duties. Carr is easygoing, works well with students, is innovative, and is skilled at building relationships.

Carr was not searching for a new job when the search firm invited him to apply for the position. He was interested because he grew up in the region and the portfolio described in the proposal was robust. The position announcement described a division of student affairs with 20 departments, a budget of more than $20 million, and major opportunities to effect institutional change to benefit students. He interviewed well and received high ratings from students and board members; faculty were lukewarm because he did not have as much teaching and research experience as they would have preferred. The search committee forwarded Carr's name to Grant as their highest rated finalist. Grant offered Carr the position and he accepted.

Before his arrival, Carr contacted all the directors in the Division of Student Affairs, using the organization chart in the position announcement. He e-mailed them, saying, "I look forward to working with each of you and staff members in your departments. I have asked my administrative assistant to contact you in the coming days to schedule some time for us to talk for a few minutes via phone. I am interested in getting to know you, introducing myself further, and hearing about your highest priorities. This will help us hit the ground running when I arrive on campus in a few short months. Thank you in advance for your time. I look forward to our conversation."

A few directors responded almost immediately, but the others did not respond at all and were reluctant to schedule appointments to talk on the phone. When Carr arrived on campus a few months later, one of the first things he wanted to do was meet with all 20 directors in his portfolio.

On his third day at Northern University, Carr received a call from Provost Mary Moore. "Hey, welcome aboard! We are delighted to have you at Northern. You are going to love it here, and I look forward to grabbing a bite to eat with you. I called to give you a heads up about a few things. I have received word from some of our staff members that you are attempting to arrange appointments to meet with them."

"That is correct," Carr said. "I would like to meet the directors in the Division of Student Affairs as soon as possible so we can begin building relationships and talking strategy for the upcoming year."

"Well, this is a little complicated," Moore replied. "The directors you have contacted are not in the Division of Student Affairs."

"Oh, I am sorry," Carr said. "I must have the wrong list."

"Well, you probably have the correct names and contact information, but those departments do not report to the Division of Student Affairs," Moore said.

"I got the list from the position description for the vice president for student affairs," Carr responded.

"I know," Moore said. "That is the problem. The position description is inaccurate. Most of those departments are still in academic affairs and auxiliary services. The search firm crafted the position description using a previous version of the division in an effort to attract high-caliber candidates. Arrangements were never made internally to transition those departments back to student affairs. Maybe we can negotiate for a couple of them to go back, but faculty members are adamant about their role in departments that are currently part of academic affairs. These departments have been under our supervision for more than 5 years, and people are reluctant to change that. For example, when student affairs had new student orientation, it was viewed as fun and games; now it is much more academic. We do not want to see that reversed."

Andy Carr's Dilemma

Carr was shocked to realize that he had been led to believe this position had greater responsibility and scope than his previous position when, in truth, it had much less of both. His new portfolio included five departments: the student center, student activities, campus recreation, student leadership programs, and the community service office. The budget and personnel numbers cited in the position description were a fraction of what he actually had, and he had no assistant vice presidents, administrative support, or office budget. He had assumed these things were in place and did not inquire about them during the interview process. He did not think to ask during the interview, "Is this position description accurate? What is the real budget for the division? Do I have administrative support?" He trusted that what was in writing was accurate. He realized too late that Northern University had reestablished the position of vice president for student affairs but had not renegotiated the return of the departments that previously made up the division. Because the position had been vacant for more than 5 years, the budget had been reallocated. The search firm decided that, to attract the best candidates, it needed a robust position description; it expected the institution to navigate the internal politics to return those departments back to the Division of Student Affairs. Many people at Northern University were aware of the discrepancies in the position description and had focused on protecting their own portfolios in preparation for the arrival of the unsuspecting new vice president.

"I have made a terrible mistake," Carr thought. "I accepted a position that has less responsibility than my previous one, and I left a job where I was challenged and appreciated to accept a position where I have been marginalized and lied to."

Should he leave and hope to recapture his old job? Should he complain to the president about the discrepancy between the job description and the actual position? Should he get into a bitter negotiation with Moore to reclaim the departments that belong in his portfolio? Should he file a complaint against the university for false advertising? Carr knows that he is at the beginning of his tenure at Northern University and that every action he takes will be observed under a microscope. If he starts his tenure by fighting for position, that could send the message that he means business or that he is overly aggressive; if he, temporarily at least, forfeits the portfolio as described in the position description, he could be viewed as a pushover or a team player and negotiator. What should he do?

Response by Brandi Hephner LaBanc, Vice Chancellor for Student Affairs, University of Mississippi

Carr is in a precarious situation and must make some quick, thoughtful decisions regarding his future. He accepted a position and uprooted his family on the basis of an exaggerated position description. He has to clear his head, evaluate his options, and commit to a plan of action. Anybody would be upset or enraged if this happened to them. Carr must remain calm and understand that finding a remedy to this situation may take longer than expected. Patience and a level head is key.

Carr has three options: (1) return to his previous institution, (2) resign and launch another job search, or (3) remain at Northern University. Each option presents different levels of risk and reward, and each must be evaluated according to his personal situation. What is the financial and emotional impact on his family in each scenario? No career decision is worth negatively affecting one's family and personal life.

Option A: Return to Former Institution

Suppose Carr decides to leave Northern University and return to his former institution. If his previous position is still available and they can fit him back into the organization, he should strongly explore this possibility. If he decides to return to his previous position, he should do so with some sensitivity to Northern University. Although in this situation some people might be tempted to walk out without regard for Northern, the professional network in higher education is too small to take that risk. Leaders are judged on how they handle challenging situations; their actions are a reflection of their character and principles. If Carr reacts impulsively or insensitively, he is at risk of damaging his own hard-earned professional reputation. His departure will affect the people who invested time in the search process, the division's employees, students, and the institutional leadership.

If he takes this route, he should be as transparent as possible and avoid doing anything that could be perceived as slanderous or damaging to Northern University's reputation. He should work with both universities to make the transition back to his previous role swift and seamless. If possible, Carr should personally share his decision to depart with colleagues and students. The communique should be forthright but supportive of Northern's leadership moving forward. A negative message or one that casts blame will only result in damaging public relations—for Carr and Northern University alike. Carr should deliver this message and move on immediately; delaying the transition or dragging out the discussion is not productive for anyone involved.

After some consideration, Carr may determine that this option has the potential to damage his professional reputation and may not be an ideal route. A leader's reputation is critical to his effectiveness on campus and beyond. To date, Carr has had a successful career in student affairs. He has achieved upward mobility, a faculty appointment, and most recently was recruited to a second chief student affairs officer role. Carr is known as an easygoing, effective administrator with strong relationship-building skills. If leaving the job at Northern creates too much negative attention, he might find that his reputation tarnished overnight. Colleagues in the tightly woven circles of student affairs will hear about his appointment and quick departure. There is a real risk that if the full story is not apparent, many people will speculate or, worse yet, rewrite the story in a negative light. There is also the nature of the Internet and social media to consider: If Carr is unable to control the publicity related to his decision in a purposeful and transparent way, negative headlines, blogs, and posts are a reality.

Option B: Resign and Launch a Search

If Carr decides to resign and launch a search for a new position, he faces the possibility of extended unemployment. He should immediately begin to tap into his professional networks and reach out to search firms to identify employment opportunities. Although this may be the riskiest move, it may make sense if staying at Northern University is unbearable and returning to his previous campus is not an option.

For any number of reasons, senior-level administrators should always be prepared for the possibility of being unexpectedly unemployed (e.g., presidential transition, downsizing, philosophy changes related to student affairs). Senior leadership roles can be volatile, so professionals should prepare themselves by maintaining at least a 3-month personal financial reserve, keeping a reasonable psychological distance from their job, and maintaining a strong professional network. Until he finds another position, Carr might consider short-term consulting, serving in an interim position at another university, or transitioning to a faculty role for a year.

In this situation, some people might consider launching a search immediately while remaining on the job, but this approach creates additional challenges. By resigning first, Carr has the option of not including this position on his résumé, as his service to the university is essentially null and void. If he does not resign and proceeds with a search, he will have to explain why he's looking for a job so soon after accepting a new position. In any case, once he qualifies for another position and moves along in the search process, he will face scrutiny regarding the short tenure in this current job. He will have to consider these issues as he decides what course of action to take.

Option C: Remain at Northern University

A third option is to stay at Northern University. If he does this, Carr must turn his attention to the president and the provost. He could ask Grant to reflect back on his listening tour, when he made the decision to return to a traditional vice president for student affairs model. Carr should use this frame of reference to work with the president to determine what went wrong and how things can be put back on track. It would serve Carr well to learn more about that listening tour and the key reasons for Grant's decision. These details should be shared with the provost in an effort to shift her perspective about the direction of student affairs. With the support of the president and the cooperation of the provost, a measured approach to returning student affairs to the traditional model is achievable. If he approaches Grant with this plan, Carr should be prepared for the possibility that the president will not take action to address the situation.

If he decides to stay, Carr must learn the historical context and culture of student affairs at Northern University. He should carefully and strategically build relationships with faculty and students—establishing a student advisory council and attending faculty senate meetings will help build these partnerships. He should adopt a data-driven approach and share division outcomes with all stakeholders. The faculty must see the scholar-practitioner in him, and students will want to hear how he will be an advocate for them.

Northern University needs a leader who can bridge the gap between the educational and auxiliary mindset and can highlight the difference between student *service* professionals and student *development* professionals. Carr's experiences in college administration make him the perfect person to forge meaningful relationships with faculty and demonstrate how critical student affairs is to Northern University. Carr is facing a challenge, but he also has an opportunity to transform the face of student affairs at Northern University. He must be innovative and infuse that trait in his daily management of the division. With the appropriate disposition and a patient approach, Carr can transform the Division of Student Affairs at Northern University.

Response by Arthur Sandeen, Former Vice President for Student Affairs, University of Florida

Carr is in a difficult situation: He accepted a position under false pretenses and now has to decide on his response. He should have known something was wrong during the interview process—it is likely there were signs in his conversations with others and his homework on the institution that something was not in order—but for whatever reason, he did not sniff out the deception. His response to this situation is complicated by the fact that he has moved his family, is a new vice president, and probably does not want to start off his tenure in conflict with his new boss and colleagues. At the same time, he has to do something in response. The question is what should he do?

Seek External Advice

In difficult situations like this one, it is wise to consider advice from long-time colleagues and friends. These conversations will be helpful as Carr decides how to proceed. Any advisors must be concerned about Carr's welfare and willing to give advice from an objective perspective. Carr has to seek advice from advisors outside the situation, where he can vent his frustration and not taint his current employment situation. He accepted the position; there has been a misunderstanding about the position responsibilities; and he needs help deciding what to do next. During these initial, upsetting weeks in his position at Northern, Carr might find it helpful to air his frustrations with friends/colleagues outside the institution, and he must make sure to take care of himself.

Don't Blame Yourself

Carr is an experienced and successful student affairs professional who is admired and respected in the field. Northern University is fortunate to have him in this leadership position. With his skills in identifying problems and building good programs and relationships, he can exceed their expectations. He has done this before at other institutions, and he can do it again. Yet, he probably wonders how he found himself in this awkward situation. His communication skills have always been excellent, and he makes it a point with staff and students to be clear about what he says and does. That said, my initial admonition to Carr is "Don't blame yourself!" That could easily trigger a downward spiral of self-doubt and second guessing; eventually he could even lose confidence in his ability to lead and to effectively make change.

Meet With the President

Carr should meet with the president as soon as he can. A vice president's relationship with the president is the most important aspect of his job. Maintaining positive, honest, and open communication with the president is extremely important. Carr should think back on when he met with the president during the interview process. What did the president say about his expectations for the new student affairs leader and the division? Northern has a very uneven history in student affairs during the past 5 years, and hiring Carr represented a new commitment to bring consistency to the division. However, an initial meeting with the president is not the time for a confrontation, so Carr should practice what he is going to say with a friend and think about how he will contain his frustration. Meeting with the president is the logical place to start. The president has the authority to correct this misunderstanding, although whether he is willing to do so is another story. Carr should concentrate his efforts on coming to an agreement with the president, his boss. It is the president who hired him and to whom he reports, and it is the president's responsibility to clarify his portfolio.

Talk to Your Predecessor

Carr should find a way to talk at length with his predecessor, Walter Wright. In fact, Carr should have had this conversation before accepting the position at Northern. If Carr took the time to invite Wright to share his experience, he could offer meaningful insight to at least help Carr establish context for the operating culture. Apparently, the situation at Northern changed enough to induce Wright to step down from the position; his decision holds important clues about the culture at Northern and what Carr might experience in his efforts to solve this problem. Although Carr's experience is not directly tied to that of Walter Wright, there is always valuable information to be learned from those who came before. Carr should take advantage of whatever knowledge he can glean from Wright and use it to his advantage.

Meet With the Provost

Mary Moore, the chief academic officer, is a key participant in this scenario. During Carr's first meeting with her, he was wise not to provoke an unprofessional confrontation—lose his temper, demand the return of his departments, make threats he could not follow up on. From an outsider's perspective, it appears that Moore may have used the opportunity of a vacant vice presidency in student affairs to enhance her own portfolio, while claiming it was the faculty that are driving the situation. (These tactics have a way of eventually weakening, not strengthening, a leader's position and influence.) As soon as the position description was posted, Moore knew it was inaccurate and that the incumbent would not be pleased with the deception, yet she did nothing to correct it before Carr's arrival. Carr was wise not to confront Moore, because it will not enhance his position in the argument. Again, the most appropriate person to clarify this situation is the president. The president has to tell Moore which departments are included in Carr's portfolio. She did not protest when those areas were included in the position description, so she would seem to be on shaky grounds for protesting now.

Reassure the Staff

Carr's relationship with his staff is critical. He is probably anxious about getting on with leading the division—meeting with his team and building a shared vision and expectations. This is a time of real uncertainty for them as well; they are not naïve about the situation and how things have worked at Northern. They are waiting anxiously to see how their new vice president is going to react to the deception. At this early point in Carr's tenure, it would be unwise to dump this situation on them. Some department heads may want to be out of student affairs and part of academic affairs; several weeks ago he met with all of them during on-campus interviews and had no clue about the situation. He simply does not know how deep the deception goes. The wise thing for Carr to do in the first few weeks is to assure the staff that he is looking forward to serving as vice president and working with everyone to improve student life. Since he does not know how this situation will play out, he has to lay the foundation for staying in case that is his best option.

Even in this imperfect situation, leading is still possible, and hardworking people can still get positive things done for students. Like most student affairs professionals, Carr is in this profession because he wants to make things better for students. This is probably why he chose to be a vice president. He took the position at Northern because he saw possibilities to make good things happen. He knows the field, has the skills, and knows what he needs to have in place to succeed. If he decides to stay at Northern, he can bring about the changes he desires, but it will require more patience and faith in the future than he imagined when he agreed to take the job. However, if he decides that he has no chance to win this fight, he should leave for another leadership position.

Response by Ainsley Carry, Vice Provost for Student Affairs, University of Southern California

Andy Carr is in a difficult situation. He uprooted his family, left a good job, and now finds himself in a position that was inaccurately advertised. The portfolio he actually oversees is less than half of what was advertised. The difficulty is deciding what to do next. Carr has a few options: He could ask the president to reinstate the portfolio as it was listed in the job description; he could battle with the provost to recoup departments that have been removed from the portfolio; he could threaten to pack his bags and leave unless the portfolio is reinstated as advertised; or he could find a way to make the best of the situation. The choices he makes will depend on his personal situation: finances, family needs, labor market, and impact on professional reputation. He will have to consider all these aspects in choosing a course of action.

Every Situation Has a Historical Context

The situation Carr finds himself in was developing well before his arrival. Internal power struggles among faculty, board members, and the administration predated Carr's arrival. The board, faculty, and students have long jockeyed for power; Carr got caught in the regular flow of business at Northern. Ten years earlier, the faculty saw an opportunity to take power from student affairs by suggesting that the president dismantle the division; the president did not take their advice the first time, but after the failed administration of Walter Wright, he yielded to the faculty request and dismantled the division. The circumstances that led to the current situation—meddling board, power-hungry faculty, and mismanagement by the previous vice president—were in motion years before Carr's arrival. This situation is less about him and more about the dysfunctional nature of the institution. Falsely advertising a position to lure top-notch candidates and not sorting out the organization chart before posting the position description is simply unprofessional and unethical, but Carr has to move forward.

Own Some of the Blame

Carr is not completely blameless in this scenario. He probably did most of his homework on the institution's website: reading past issues of the student newspapers, reviewing board minutes, studying organization charts, and memorizing financial reports. A note of caution when conducting research to prepare for an interview: Information about an institution that is publicly accessible via the Internet and other news sources is only a small fraction of what candidates really need to know about their potential new employer. Institutions work hard to keep inconvenient truths off their websites. Information about organizational dysfunction and risks inherent to the position are only captured through in-depth interviews with colleagues and former employees. The Internet is a good place to glean surface information about the institution, but it is unreliable in detecting warning signs about organizational culture and hidden issues. Carr obviously did not talk to people associated with Northern. He should have interviewed former employees, asked colleagues questions about the institution's reputation, requested a list of references, and found ways during the recruitment period to dig deeper into the organizational culture and hidden issues. The Internet is a good source of information, but in the context of evaluating an organization it is limited by its lack of ability to communicate culture and hidden issues.

Carr missed obvious warning signs. Chances are his desire to succeed in the interview process and advance his career blinded him to clues about the division's structure. During the interviews, he should have noticed who was listed on the interview itinerary and connected with potential direct reports. If half of the direct reports were not on the interview itinerary, that should have raised a question, and he should have asked why. He also should have asked probing questions about his areas to learn more about their strengths, weaknesses, and needs; if no answers were forthcoming, this should have been a clue. Carr should have used the search consultant to garner information about the division and to probe deeper. It appears that he wanted to advance his career so badly that he was vulnerable during the search process. He wanted the job so much that he ignored warning signs and did not ask critical questions about the division.

Deal With Emotions

Before deciding on any options, Carr needs to work on his own feelings. He has been duped. He is probably angry and feels betrayed. Looking back on the interview process, he probably sees all the warning signs and wonders why he did not pick up on what was going on—this only makes him more upset. The truth is, he wanted the job. It appeared to be a promotion and a great chance to advance his career. Under those circumstances, it was easy to ignore subtle discrepancies and trust that things would work themselves out, but recognizing this doesn't mitigate the anger and hurt he feels. Carr has to manage his emotions before he can make a sound decision on next steps. If he elects to stay, he has to put his feelings behind him and move forward. If he elects to leave, he cannot let this betrayal permeate future interviews, because hiring committees are likely to reject candidates who show signs of bitterness toward previous employers. Stay or leave, Carr has to get past the anger.

Make Lemonade

At this point, the most important question for Carr is what to do next. His options include fighting for what was outlined in the position description, ignoring the deception, or doing his best work for 1 year, then leaving at the first opportunity. Another option is a combination of the three. Carr should request a meeting with the president and provost to let them know that he wants the situation to be corrected. He has a good case in (1) the lack of integrity reflected in the position description, and (2) the need for holistic student development through the full series of departments that were outlined in the position description. This is not a meeting to make threats, but Carr must state for the record that he wants the discrepancy corrected. This is not a fight, it is a discussion among mature professionals; Carr must contain his emotions and speak with a clear head. Fighting with the president and provost during the transition period is not how a new vice president for student affairs wants to start his tenure.

Regardless of what happens in the meeting with the president and the provost, Carr has to direct the attention of his leadership team and division toward moving forward. Rather than dwelling on the past and on how he feels, he has to find a way to convince the division that this is not a bad situation and they can make it work to their advantage. Everyone knows what happened. They all saw the position description and wondered if those areas would return to the division. Now they recognize the deception, and everyone is waiting to see how Carr will react. He should acknowledge the deception but focus on moving the division forward by posing this question to his leadership team: "Should we spend the next year fighting for the old portfolio or think about what the future could look like and where we should invest our time and energy?" Carr has to convince his leadership team that this is the best option and energize them to imagine the possibilities for the future.

Chapter Summary

In this case study, Andy Carr was deceived by a hiring process that included an inflated and inaccurate position description for vice president for student affairs. When he assumed the position, Carr learned that the scope of the job was grossly exaggerated. The core issue is dealing with a change in expectations during the transition process. Three vice presidents offer advice.

- 🔵 Evaluate all options. Brandi Hephner LaBanc suggests that Carr could (1) return to his former institution, (2) resign from the new position and begin a search for a new position, or (3) remain at Northern University. Each option has pros and cons; all should be evaluated first according to personal and family priorities.

- 🔵 Seek advice from friends and colleagues outside the institution. Transitioning to a new position has its fair share of personal and institutional stressors, but complaining about the job will send the wrong message to everyone at the institution, from the president to students. Carr needs a circle of friends and colleagues outside the institution with whom he can vent his frustrations and discuss strategies to deal with the problem.

- Discuss the problem with the president as soon as possible. Meet with the president to discuss expectations, opportunities, and resource needs. He was hired by the president, reports to the president, and has to meet the president's expectations. Carr's situation could be an oversight that is easily corrected or it could have been a plot to attract a talented candidate; he needs to get to the bottom of it with his boss, the president.

- Reassure the staff about his commitment to the division. Staff members know what is going on. When they read the position description, they saw that the portfolio was misrepresented. Now they are waiting to see how the new vice president will react to the deception. Whether Carr intends to stay or leave, he should reassure them that he is committed to moving the division forward. If he decides to stay, he will be glad that he built a foundation of trust with the staff.

- Neutralize emotions. Anyone would be upset about this situation, but we cannot let anger dictate how we communicate. Communicating in anger distracts from the message and will fall on deaf ears. Carr should vent to friends outside the institution; on the job, he should focus on communicating with calmness and clarity. He should ensure that the issues take center stage rather than his feelings about them.

- Make the most of a bad situation. Carr should consider the positive aspects of the situation. This is a chance to completely rethink his division. The field is constantly evolving—new ideas and opportunities emerge every year, and new programs and services develop as students' needs change. Instead of worrying about the former portfolio, Carr should focus on creating new opportunities, investing in making the departments in the portfolio outstanding, and building a professional brand.

The Internal Candidate

Ainsley Carry, Arthur Sandeen,
Mary B. Coburn, and Felecia J. Lee

Patricia Thompson is the new vice president for student affairs at Orange University. She took over the reins from the legendary Vice President Alex Snow. Snow served Orange University for 30 years; he groomed all the senior staff members who remain in the division. Snow's most devoted protégé, Mark Riley, is the associate vice president and dean of students. Riley was an internal candidate for the vice presidency, but the president selected Thompson because of her breadth and depth of experience. Riley is unhappy and plans to undermine Thompson's efforts in hopes that she will be fired and he will be the savior.

Institutional Background

Orange University is a midsized, state-funded institution on the West Coast of the United States. Founded in 1905, it offers a full complement of academic degree programs in seven schools and colleges and two professional schools. More than 30,000 students are enrolled; more then 60 percent of the student body is in-state, 70 percent is White, 25 percent is

Black, and 5 percent is international and other races. The university enjoys stability in senior leadership and strong support from the board of trustees and state legislators. The current president has been at Orange University for less than 5 years, while the provost and general counsel have been there for more than 15 years. Orange University is the state's largest employer and number one producer of teachers, engineers, and business leaders. The university suffered through periods of instability and tension under the previous presidential administration; stability and prosperity have replaced stress and anxiety under the current president. In the past, decisions were made without consensus and staff members were uncertain about personnel changes. The current president—an innovative leader with a hands-off leadership style—has established an atmosphere of tranquility.

Division of Student Affairs Background

The vice president for student affairs reports directly to the president. Departments in the portfolio include student activities, Greek life, student conduct, student center, counseling services, recreation center, leadership programs, orientation, student infirmary, financial aid, registration, enrollment services, university housing, dining, transportation, and public safety. Alex Snow, the former vice president for student affairs, had divided the portfolio between the associate vice president and dean of students, Mark Riley, and the assistant vice president, Yvonne Young. More than 75 percent of the division reported to Riley. Snow supervised Riley and Young, and oversaw the development office, assessment office, and parent programs.

Snow is a legend in the student affairs profession. He is nationally known through his research, publications, and work with professional associations. He has mentored hundreds of professionals and graduate students who have gone on to become deans and vice presidents. After serving as dean of students at Clover College, Snow was asked by his president to come with him when he accepted the presidency at Orange University. Snow was 33 years old when he came onboard as vice president for student affairs; he has stayed more than 30 years.

Riley was hired into the Division of Student Affairs straight out of the graduate program at Orange University. He was an active student leader as an undergraduate, earned high marks in his graduate courses, and did impressive work for the division as a graduate assistant. When an entry-level position opened up, he applied and was hired. Although Riley reported to one of Snow's direct reports, Snow took a special interest in him. The two published together and made professional presentations, and Snow convinced Riley to pursue a doctorate in higher education administration. Over 15 years, Riley was promoted internally to progressively more responsible positions until he became the associate vice president and dean of students.

For more than 20 years, Riley was educated and groomed to be a student affairs professional at Orange University, and he was mentored by one of the best in the business. He had a good reputation outside the division but was not well-liked by his colleagues, who knew him well and had concerns about his maturity and scope of experience. Riley had spent his entire career at Orange University under the protection of Snow. He was considered to be "Snow's boy"; thus, no one ever confronted him, and he received no feedback from others about his immaturity or his abrasive and condescending management style. He used his relationship with Snow to threaten others into compliance, which was how he got things done. Rather than complain, some employees simply left the division. Snow protected Riley from political drama and tough management decisions, so he did not develop people skills to go along with his leadership responsibilities.

When Snow announced his retirement, Riley assumed that he was the obvious choice to replace his mentor and began actively politicking for the position. Outside the Division of Student Affairs he enjoyed a lot of support; few knew him well, but they saw him as a person who got things done. Internally, a number of staff members vowed to leave or retire if Riley was selected as the next vice president. At this point, many staff members went to Snow privately to warn him about anointing Riley as his successor. Snow was surprised to hear some of the disparaging remarks about his protégé, but he listened carefully. Before leaving, Snow gave Riley the feedback he had received from staff members in the division; Riley later lost his cool with some of his direct reports for talking behind his back.

The president used a reputable search firm to conduct a national search for the new vice president for student affairs. The expectations for this role had expanded during Snow's administration; anyone who did not meet these expectations would not be successful. Riley applied for the position with full confidence that he would be the successful candidate. He assumed that no one knew more than he did about the position and the issues, and that his years with Snow would give him an edge over external candidates. More than 80 candidates applied, 10 received phone interviews, and 4 were invited for on-campus interviews. The committee offered Riley an on-campus interview out of courtesy but did not consider him a legitimate candidate because of his lack of experience outside Orange University. After a semester-long national search process, the president selected Patricia Thompson as the next vice president for student affairs.

Patricia Thompson's Background

Patricia Thompson is an Ivy League graduate with stellar academic credentials from three top-ranked institutions of higher education. She is widely published and has served on a number of national and local committees. She earned her bachelor's degree in psychology, master's in counseling, and doctorate in higher education administration. She also has a master's degree in business administration. All her degrees are from top-tier institutions. Thompson's 25 years of experience at five different institutions includes teaching roles in colleges of business and education, a stint in state government as a university lobbyist, and work in university fundraising and development. Most recently she was vice president for student affairs at a large public institution. Her interviews were flawless and her professionalism second to none. The committee was unanimous in selecting her as the most talented candidate—she brought broad experience to the position and represented the best chance for forward progress. The president wanted fresh ideas and a bold new vision for student affairs. He and the search committee believed that Thompson was better equipped to deliver on this vision than any other candidate.

Patricia Thompson's Dilemma

Riley was devastated by the decision. He was certain he was the best person for the position and believed that he had been groomed for it for the past 20 years. He felt betrayed by his colleagues in the division who provided negative feedback during the last days of Snow's tenure. He was sure this feedback had made its way to the search committee and resulted in his not getting the position. He believed that the president should have considered his years of dutiful service to Orange University rather than relying on the jealous comments of uninformed colleagues. Although he had not met her, Riley despised Thompson for taking the job away from him. He considered resigning in protest but realized that would only hurt him. He took a week off from work to contemplate his future. During this time, he came up with a plan.

Thompson arrived at Orange University in June and received a heartfelt welcome from the university community and members of her staff. The president introduced her at a universitywide reception in the student center; hundreds were in attendance. The president bragged about her credentials and how lucky Orange University was to have her. He showered her with praise and let everyone know that she was his top choice. A student group performed the school song and presented Thompson with school paraphernalia. Staff members welcomed her with gifts and good wishes. Former Vice President Snow offered his continued support. Thompson was overwhelmed by the generosity and kind words, and graciously thanked the president and all speakers for their remarks. Thompson said, "I look forward to working with all of you to continue the great work former Vice President Snow started. I am delighted to be here."

Riley stood in the back of the room and watched everything without cracking a smile or applauding. He was visibly upset. He said to a colleague,

"This entire spectacle makes me sick to my stomach." Riley's plan was to spend the next year undermining Thompson's efforts. He was convinced that she was not the right person for the job. His plan was to make her look bad enough that she would eventually be fired and he would be the savior. He planned to discredit her with employees outside the division; in fact, he went so far as to do his own background checks on her. He called employees at her previous institutions, looking for scandalous information about her; when he could not find anything, he made up stories and leaked them to others. He vowed not to offer any information that might help her; in fact, he would provide inaccurate information to send her down the wrong path.

Thompson, one of the most astute professionals in college administration, read Riley from the beginning and suspected that he would be an obstruction rather than an ally. She was aware that he had been an internal candidate and had been groomed over many years by her predecessor. No one specifically warned her about Riley's disposition and his reaction to not being selected, but she could tell by his behavior and frequent absences that something was not right.

For the first 4 weeks of Thompson's tenure, Riley kept his distance. He took several days of vacation, and when he came back he stayed out of his office as much as possible. He avoided one-on-one meetings with her and sat at the far end of the conference table during staff meetings. Finally Thompson scheduled a 2-hour meeting with Riley to get to know him and establish a plan for restructuring the division. More than 75 percent of the division reported to Riley, and Thompson wanted to balance things out between him and Yvonne Young, the assistant vice president. Her intention was to win Riley over and bring him on board. For the first 30 minutes, the two exchanged pleasantries and shared their stories in an effort to get to know one another.

Then Thompson said, "Now, I would like to talk about how we can work together to move the division forward. You have been a valued member of this team for many years, and I look forward to working with you to do what is best for students and staff. Can I count on you to work with me?"

"Of course you can count on me," Riley said. "We have the same goal: student success."

"Good," Thompson said. "Let's talk about how we might structure the division to create more balance between you and the other assistant vice president."

"Well, I am the *associate* vice president and dean of students," Riley replied. "I think the portfolio is appropriately structured, and I am hoping that we are not going to change anything this year. How about we just operate as we are and give you time to settle in? Then maybe next year we talk about structural changes. I am hoping my portfolio does not change. My direct reports are very devoted to me."

"Mark, you are going to have to meet me halfway," Thompson said. "There are some structural things that need to be changed, and I have scheduled enough time today for us to exchange ideas that will create opportunities for both of us. I want to hear your ideas. This is just a brainstorming session, and we have time to imagine."

"Speaking of time, I forgot that I have a meeting I need to run to," Riley said. "I am going to have to reschedule. I am sorry, I forgot about this other meeting."

Thompson was shocked as he stood up to excuse himself 30 minutes into their 2-hour meeting. "Mark, we scheduled this meeting over 2 weeks ago," she said. "We need to talk about these things. I would prefer to move forward together, but I have no problem making these decisions on my own."

"I am sorry, but I really have to head to this other meeting. I am late," Riley said as he left Thompson's office.

Response by Mary Coburn, Vice President for Student Affairs, Florida State University

Inheriting a staff member who hoped to get the job him- or herself is one of the more difficult challenges a new vice president for student affairs can face. In the best of circumstances, you will have a strong staff member who is disappointed but can recover to become a contributing member of the team. This case study demonstrates the other extreme: a bitter, immature, and vengeful staff member whose actions show why he would not have been a good choice for the position.

Handling this situation successfully will require a multifaceted strategy involving the president and senior leadership, human resources, student affairs senior staff, possibly the former vice president, and Riley himself.

Meet With the President and Senior Leadership

The support of the university president is crucial throughout the process. The president must be made aware of Riley's resistance and lack of cooperation. Thompson should tell the president that she intends to handle the situation, but she did not want him to hear about it through the rumor mill. She should promise to keep him informed. Depending on the relationships she has already built with her fellow vice presidents, she may talk with them about the situation. She can ask if they have heard rumors or if they have had any experiences with Riley that might be instructive. Their support could be important.

Meet With Human Resources

Thompson needs to become familiar with the university's human resources policies to determine her options. Handling the situation between colleagues would be the best alternative, but it is possible that Riley could use his knowledge to misinform her. She needs to be aware of resources and alternatives available through human resources, including employee improvement plans, discipline, reassignment, reorganization, grievance procedures, contract nonrenewal, and immediate dismissal.

Meet With Student Affairs Staff

Regardless of the climate in the division, any new vice president should become acquainted as quickly as possible with senior leaders and middle managers. In this case, Thompson especially needs to get to know

Riley's direct reports. Ideally, she can arrange individual meetings to get feedback and ideas about where the division has been and where it needs to go. In addition to being informative, these meetings will help Thompson evaluate staff allegiance. Who is onboard and who might be siding with Riley? If staff are open, these meetings will help her gather information about Riley—past issues, preferred strategies, allies, and detractors.

Meet With the Former Vice President

Given the small world of student affairs, Thompson may already be acquainted with her predecessor. Snow is highly respected and has a national reputation, so meeting with him could be instructive on several fronts. His insights and assessment of the state of the division could be helpful. Soliciting his evaluation of Riley's strengths and weaknesses might give Thompson the opportunity to share her observations. It is important to be honest about what she has experienced but to state it in the most positive terms, knowing that anything she says might be passed on to Riley. If Thompson is clear about her intention not to tolerate staff insubordination, Snow might help mentor Riley into a more positive and realistic state. Snow might also advise Riley that it is time for him to explore other options: Strengthening his credentials with experience elsewhere could help him eventually become vice president for student affairs at Orange or another institution.

Meet With Mark Riley

Thompson should address Riley directly. If he will not schedule a meeting with her, his assistant can identify free time, or Thompson can just walk into his office and close the door. She should be direct and clear about her awareness of his ongoing efforts to avoid meeting with her and should tell him that this is not acceptable. Then she should deliver the feedback she has gathered about his management style and his reputation with colleagues in the division. She can describe her broad goals for the division and the strategies she will implement to achieve them. She can outline her plan to evaluate the organization chart and staff portfolios of responsibilities to increase productivity and effectiveness. In order to do this, she can tell Riley that she will expect a climate that is open, supportive, collaborative, and team-oriented. She should describe her expectations for his performance and cooperation. Then, depending on the advice she received from human resources experts, she can directly address the consequences of further insubordination—misinformation, lack of cooperation, or undermining the division's goals. She might say, "If I find that a staff member is working counter to our stated goals, I will be forced to pursue all options available under university policy, including dismissal." She can list the options she is willing to entertain: reprimand, reassignment, suspension, or dismissal. To make sure Riley cannot claim later that he did not understand the message, Thompson should bring a document summarizing her message in writing and have him sign a copy.

If Thompson uses this multifaceted approach, Riley should clearly understand that she will not tolerate his insubordination. If he persists in his misconduct, she should not hesitate to employ the full range of options available through human resources. In addition to resolving the Riley situation, her firm direction will send a message to the division about her values and expectations. If he has been bullying staff members, they will appreciate her actions and she will gain their loyalty. In addition, any other staff who may be underperforming will receive a clear message about her expectations.

Response by Arthur Sandeen, Former Vice President for Student Affairs, University of Florida

Thompson is probably eager to move forward in her new position, honoring the past accomplishments of the Division of Student Affairs but also bringing fresh new approaches, ideas, and programs. Her transition has encountered a significant obstacle in Mark Riley, the associate vice president and dean of students. Riley has been at Orange for many years and is unhappy that he was not selected to be vice president. Since Thompson's appointment, he has been uncooperative and has fomented unrest among the staff.

Do Not Get Angry

It would be reasonable for Thompson to be angry at having to start her new position with this type of opposition. She does not want Riley to prevent her from moving ahead with her plans. It is okay for her to get angry, but it is never a good idea to make important decisions from this perspective. She was chosen for this position because she has been a successful leader. Riley would be resentful and nasty to anyone appointed to the position, which he wanted for himself. Thompson has to take time before she decides what she is going to do. She is likely to make better decisions when she is not angry.

Thompson showed a commendable ability to remain calm during her first meeting with Riley. Riley displayed an unprofessional and nonsupportive attitude, while Thompson stayed on task with her objectives for the meeting. She did not flinch when he directly challenged her authority, announced his own priorities, and ended the meeting. Thompson was wise not to confront him at that time and did not fret when he left her office. She needs to take time to process the meeting and formulate a plan to deal with the situation, to make decisions not in anger but after thoughtful consideration.

Be Patient

Personnel challenges are often the most difficult to resolve, and resolution always takes longer than expected. Riley has shown clearly that he does not intend to be an asset to the Division of Student Affairs; in fact, he plans to be a significant distraction. Thompson is correct in her assessment that his attitude and actions are challenging her leadership and will negatively affect staff and students. Riley's insubordination is grounds for termination, and Thompson has the right to proceed along that path, working with human resources to devise a plan. This is where patience is crucial. Among their many responsibilities, human resources departments protect the university from wrongful termination claims; properly dismissing an employee takes time and patience. To do it right, a number of steps must be followed: documentation, disciplinary meetings, performance evaluations, and more disciplinary meetings. This is a tremendous burden to take on during a transition, but allowing the problem to linger will only result in bigger problems later.

Talk to a Friend

A major challenge for new vice presidents is that they do not yet have trusted confidants on campus with whom they can openly and honestly share ideas, frustrations, and plans. Being new, they do not know whom to trust and where to process difficult scenarios. Thus, they tend to retreat into themselves and make decisions on their own—decisions that do not have the benefit of multiple perspectives. Often, they regret decisions made this way. Thompson needs to talk this situation through with a colleague who is not employed at Orange University and not emotionally connected to the situation. She has to get another view on the problem; not someone who will agree with her, but someone who can provide critical perspective. She might come to the same conclusion—terminate Mark Riley—but the process of seeking a different perspective will strengthen her position.

Follow the Process

Chances are that Riley will eventually accept another position, resign, or be terminated. Thompson must be sure to follow the process outlined by human resources; otherwise, the situation could come back to haunt her. She should keep the president in the loop. When Riley's future at the university has been decided, Thompson should immediately call a staff meeting to announce it. She should not discuss the specific decision, mentioning only that Riley will release a statement. Thompson should write a public statement for the information office to distribute, thanking Riley for his years of service to the institution. Finally, she should meet with student leaders to share the news directly, still refraining from divulging any details.

Terminating a longtime staff member is never easy, but Thompson's transition to the vice presidency will not be successful with Riley as associate vice president and dean of students. His continued presence on the staff will only result in distrust, angst, and a lack of progress toward Thompson's goals for the division. She could have waited and placed Riley on probation, hoping his behavior would change and he would become a valuable team player, but in the interest of the Division of Student Affairs and her own transition success, Thompson had to act sooner rather than later.

To be successful at Orange University, Thompson needs to establish her own identity and earn the respect of staff, students, the president, and the community. She is fortunate to have followed a legendary vice president such as Snow, but she cannot be an extension of him; she has to build her own brand and let people know she will do things differently. It will take time for everyone to adjust to Thompson as vice president, but as long as she stays the course, remains confident, and moves ahead, she will enjoy her tenure at Orange University.

Response by Felicia J. Lee, Assistant Vice Chancellor and Chief of Staff, University of California, Berkley

Everyone reading this case wants to shout "You're fired!" to Mark Riley and dismiss him for insubordination. But as a vice president, Patricia Thompson knows that is not the path forward—not immediately, anyway. Thompson is in the grip of emotions she cannot fully comprehend, because she does not have enough substantive information about him. It is impossible for her to grasp the underlying causes and motivations for his over-the-top behavior. Furthermore, she is experiencing her own emotions in response to Riley's behavior: confusion, frustration, and anger. In addition, she just assumed a high-profile position and is dealing with the stressors and challenges inherent in major job transitions.

Seek Counsel and Align Your Values

Thompson would benefit from seeking diverse counsel regarding her interactions with Riley. She would be wise to thread the best pearls of wisdom from multiple sources (internal and external) to construct a balanced, creative, and compassionate course of action. I use the word *compassionate* to underscore the point that Riley's behavior, however unconscionable, is most likely rooted in pain and shock. In matters of the heart—which is what Thompson is dealing with at its core, not just unprofessional behavior—a nuanced and artistic strategy is generally more effective than a rational human resources approach.

Often when we need to execute a difficult personnel action, it is easier for us to dehumanize the person. For some, this provides a justification for taking actions that are contrary to their values. Too many senior executives have looked in the rearview mirror of their careers and realized that they would have handled challenging employees differently if they had managed their own feelings first and ensured that they engaged the individual(s) in a manner congruent with their own values. There is no perfect formula for dealing with the human condition, which leads us to the next point.

Know Thyself

Through my experience as an executive coach as well as in my own administrative career path, I have learned that the most rewarding and challenging approach to an organizational problem is not to start with the "other" but to begin with the "self." Executives continue to believe that the source of conflict is external to them and that they can change others through command and control without detrimental consequences to the organization; this approach causes suffering for the leaders themselves. Thompson's most important job right now is to focus the work inward— invest time and energy in observing how she is "showing up" as the vice president. This will raise her emotional awareness and enable her to understand her behavior under duress.

One of my favorite sayings is "Your IQ (intelligence quotient) will get you the job, but your EQ (emotional intelligence) will enable you to keep it." Ironically, this is at the heart of why Riley has found himself in his current predicament. Some might think Thompson is exposing her vulnerability by seeking input, but it is a testament to her leadership skills that she asks for support and draws on her network to brainstorm a confounding issue. Asking for help is a marker of self-confidence and not, as many people think, a weakness. We are wired to be innately curious, to learn what we do not know. Thompson can learn a lot about her own leadership narrative simply by exploring her emotions, motivations, triggers, and values.

Personal and Professional Social Identities

It would be easy to move quickly to discipline Riley, to let him (and others) know who is in charge. In fact, inaction might reflect poorly on Thompson's reputation as a leader. Staff members are unforgiving toward executives who are perceived as pushovers, conflict-averse, or naïve. We all have our list of worst fears to keep at bay in order to avoid being labeled a certain type of leader. These fears are usually born of personal and professional social identities (e.g., ethnicity, age, gender, class, physical or mental ability, sexual orientation) and life experiences (e.g., past supervisors, family patterns, trauma) that solidify over time. These fears are also a response to real and perceived expectations from others, and can have a negative effect on our overall health—intellectually, physically, emotionally, and spiritually. Thompson needs to acknowledge how her professional and social identities might be contributing to her reaction to Riley's behavior.

Overreliance on Cognitive Perspective

Academic organizations often proclaim cultivation of the intellect as the highest competency. Even the student affairs profession has responded accordingly, creating rigorous cocurricular student learning outcomes and research on assessment, student development, and crisis management. These are wonderful contributions, but the profession has emulated academic leadership standards by requiring vice presidents, assistant vice presidents, and even director-level staff to have doctoral degrees. This emulation has effectively devalued and disconnected other parts of our human domains—separating intellect from emotions and emotions from physiology as sources of wisdom and information. As a result, there is an overreliance and overdependence on using cognitive perspectives to manage complex issues.

While college students are encouraged to discern, engage, and develop their whole selves, administrators have become comfortable doing the opposite. When organizational systems reward intellectually driven outputs as exclusive markers for leadership excellence, it is easy to succumb to those expectations. Fortune 500 companies (the biggest proponents of rational thought) invest millions of dollars to ensure that rising executives are taught to increase and cultivate their emotional intelligence—the ability to understand oneself and others and to use those insights to guide one's professional and personal life, and to connect with others in a positive, meaningful way. Not surprisingly, EQ affects the bottom line in a positive direction. It is now accepted that organizations succeed and fail on the basis of the integrated health profile of the people who produce the work. The recent corporate tendency to call human resources "people development" illustrates a paradigm shift and a new investment in EQ.

My Advice to Thompson

Analyze the physical response. Thompson must pause and reflect on how this situation is affecting her at every level—intellectually, physically, and emotionally. To bring her awareness to the body (reveal to herself how this situation is impacting her physically), she can ask herself questions such as: "When I think of Mark Riley or the situation, how do I feel? Am I aware of my breath? Is it shallow or deep? Am I tense or relaxed? Am I sleeping well, or do I feel exhausted? Does my nervous system flood with dread at the sight of Riley? Does my blood pressure rise simply by typing an e-mail to him?" Physical awareness will help her understand how she is absorbing the issue. She can use that knowledge to inform her response and strategy.

When we are in touch with our somatic way of being in the world, our physiological responses can teach us simple yet powerful truths. And as our reactions manifest through our physical body, others are reading us. It is like watching the president of the United States age before our eyes, even as his press secretary insists that everything is fine. Or the leader who thinks she is exuding confidence when in fact she is just talking nonstop. We might be able to convince ourselves intellectually that we are responding in a particular way, but our somatic response is a brutally honest barometer of what's really going on.

Analyze the emotional response. The next dimension for Thompson to observe is her emotional response. She can ask herself the following questions: "What am I feeling? Am I aware of any triggering tendencies or insecurities? What causes anxiety, anger, resentment, defensiveness, or fear? Why? When stressful or unforeseen situations arise, how do I handle them? What are my default patterns for coping, responding, or managing issues? Have they been effective? How can I be sure? When was the last time I had a 360 evaluation? Do I foster a culture of trust and feedback or am I the Empress With No Clothes?" In other words, am I the only one that does not know what everyone else around me knows? If Thompson sees that her strategies have been ineffective, how did that happen and what keeps her from changing her behavior?

Thompson has to get to the core of her feelings about the way Riley is behaving toward her. Are her feelings affecting her ability to be the leader she wants to be for Riley and others on campus? Executives rarely spend time trying to understand their leadership narrative—the stories they tell themselves that get in the way, cause a lot of heartache and stress, or cause them to act on inaccurate data. One's leadership narrative is an internal self-perception unconsciously used to help make decisions.

Seek clarity. I am not suggesting that Thompson enter therapy. I am suggesting that she seek clarity. There is a big difference. The last place leaders want to go is inward. It is always about how others are acting, what others are not doing, or what others are unfairly saying. Leaders must take action for accountability, divisional culture, power dynamics, and politics, but they should always start with where they are in the equation. They have to be honest in their assessment and ground themselves before they jump to a solution. Is Thompson clear on her values as a leader? If so, how will that clarity inform her response to Riley? This is where an executive coach or an unbiased advisor can help by pointing out blind spots. Everyone has them. The most courageous leaders are open to identifying gaps in their EQs and recognizing that learning and development are lifelong endeavors that do not stop at the executive level. These leaders can be spotted a mile away; their authenticity is palpable.

The more Thompson understands who she is and how this situation affects her day-to-day actions as a leader, the more confident and mindful she will be in taking the first step toward resolution.

Chapter Summary

Thompson's situation is not unusual in college administration: A long-time employee expects to step into the role of chief and becomes disgruntled when that role is given to someone else. Through no fault of his or her own, the incoming vice president has to deal with this disgruntled employee during the transition. Some new vice presidents will try to ignore the problem, but that only makes it worse. It must be resolved during the transition period. Every institution has a process for dealing with this kind of situation. Although the process varies by institution, some facets are universal:

- Follow the protocol. Responders suggested meeting with the president and with human resources experts to gather information and inform them of the situation. Involve human resources early in the process. Regardless of what Thompson intends to do—terminate, ask for a resignation, or work through the problem—she has to consult with human resources to follow the appropriate procedures. Transparency and information are crucial. Gathering the facts and keeping everyone in the loop will pay off in the end.

- Acknowledge the emotions. It is reasonable for Thompson to be angry about the way her transition is being sabotaged by a disgruntled senior staff member. Bottling up these emotions will create tension for her, but it is important for her not to make decisions in anger. She should pause and reflect on how the situation is affecting her at every level: intellectually, physically, and emotionally. She should ask herself, "When I think of Mark Riley or the situation, how do I feel?" "Am I sleeping well or do I feel exhausted?" "Does my nervous system flood with dread at the sight of him?" "Does my blood pressure rise when I type an e-mail to him?" She has to let physical awareness teach her how she is absorbing the issue, and then devise her strategy.

- Seek outside counsel and support. Contact friends and colleagues to vent frustrations. Sometimes a friend can provide another perspective or serve as a sounding board. Share your frustration with people outside the institution; this is not the time to share frustrations internally, because you do not yet know whom to trust. Opening up to the wrong person could impede your efforts to resolve the matter or reflect poorly on your judgment.

- Deal with yourself first. Dealing with transition challenges requires self-reflection. Leaders must be familiar with their own issues and narrative. Social identities and past experiences can blind people to their own roles in conflicts, to the point that the focus and the blame are always external. The ability to look inward first leads to more effective problem solving.

A Bold New Vision
But Declining Resources

Amy Hecht, Mary B. Coburn, Arthur Sandeen,
and Brandi Hephner LaBanc

Dan Marin was selected as the new vice president for student affairs and charged by the president to "create a bold new vision for student affairs." He moved swiftly, created a comprehensive strategic plan, and revised the organizational structure. Shortly after he began implementing his plan, the Division of Student Affairs faced a $3 million budget cut, which precipitated a second reorganization and the elimination of several programs. A year later, the division faced a second round of budget cuts; by this time, staff members were exhausted from the changes and budget cuts. The budget cuts threaten to undo everything Marin built in his first year.

Institutional Background

The University of the Southeast was established in the late 1880s as a coeducational state institution. In 2010, *U.S. News and World Report* ranked Southeast as one of the top public institutions in the country. Southeast enrolls 25,000 undergraduate students and 5,000 graduate students, and is led by Kathryn Perry, the university's 15th president. A Southeast alumna, Perry has promoted her vision to expand the university's academic reputation as a global institution by increasing its reach across the United States and beyond. This vision is fully supported by the board of trustees.

Division of Student Affairs Background

The Division of Student Affairs at Southeast University was led for 15 years by Vice President J. C. Smith. Smith was a warm person who focused her efforts on building teams and ensuring that staff felt comfortable in their roles. She spent the majority of her time building and maintaining relationships with staff, faculty, and students. Over the years, Smith fostered strong, positive relationships with most members of campus, including the board of trustees. Her leadership preference was to maintain the status quo rather than rock the boat. Staff described her as conflict-averse and determined to maintain harmony.

When Smith announced her retirement, President Perry conducted a national search for someone who could share her vision for the university. She did not have a specific direction in mind for the Division of Student Affairs, but she knew that student affairs could be doing more to advance the university's academic mission. The president hired Dan Marin and charged him to "Take the division apart and rebuild it with a bold new direction." The instructions lacked details, but the prospect inspired the new vice president.

The President's Charge

The president wanted to see fast results from the new vice president. Marin felt that pressure and sought to make rapid changes. During his first 6 months, he reorganized the division, established assessment protocols, and developed a strategic plan for student affairs. He formed an executive team to help with the reorganization; the team created a new organizational model with few remnants of the former model. The new model symbolized broad change, shifted a number of reporting lines, created new cluster groups, and added new departments.

Marin also began the process of developing a strategic plan. He believed the image of the Division of Student Affairs was inaccurate and did not reflect the true value of its programs and services. He knew that he needed data to demonstrate the educational outcomes of these programs and services, so he made data collection and data-informed decision making key components of the strategic plan.

Staff members had doubts about the types of changes and grew uncertain about the future. Around the water cooler and behind closed doors, they complained about changes they believed did not make sense and about the lack of communication. They felt as though they did not know what was going on and did not understand the future direction of the division.

Deep Budget Cuts

Just as the division began moving forward, the state budget office ordered the university to make a 20% budget cut; for the Division of Student Affairs, that amounted to $3 million. Marin adopted a people-first philosophy and made every effort to preserve jobs. He was committed to finding every staff member a place in the division, even if it was not in the person's current department. He looked at position vacancies and eliminated those that were not mission-critical. Then he reassigned staff members to enable mission-critical areas to function. People who retired were not replaced. Responsibilities essential to the strategic goals were reassigned. These changes gave birth to a new division structure that merged several functional areas and focused on doing more with less.

The wave of change—new vice president, new division structure, new strategic plan, and budget cuts—began wearing on the staff. The $3 million cut left the division short-staffed and employees overworked, which affected morale. Most staff members felt uneasy, anxious, and unclear about the changes. Those who were transferred felt uncertain about their new positions. Supervisors had to deal with the emotional fallout of so many changes in a once-stable division. Members of the executive team frequently dealt with questions about job security; they were careful not to make promises, as they did not know whether future budget cuts were pending.

In the next fiscal year, the university faced a second round of budget cuts. Student affairs was told to cut another $3 million from its budget. This killed all momentum that had been gained by surviving the previous budget cuts and the division restructure. Staff were certain that this round of cuts would result in layoffs, and many people expressed concern about how long the division could survive at this rate of change. One staff member said, "After a certain point, more with less is not possible. It becomes less with less." The executive team began to echo that sentiment. The bold new vision for student affairs fell victim to declining financial and human resources.

Response by Mary Coburn, Vice President for Student Affairs, Florida State University

Unfortunately, many vice presidents have faced this situation in recent years. While the wise administrator continues to seek ways to grow and achieve the vision during challenging years, multiple-year budget cuts inevitably take their toll on the ability to provide effective services to students and on staff morale. Staff can rally once in response to the need for significant reductions, but subsequent cuts tend to erode trust and make staff fearful for their jobs.

To analyze this situation and suggest steps to move forward, consider the factors that led to it. First, given the president's charge to move forward quickly to implement a new vision, how did the vice president for student affairs introduce and create the needed change? Who was involved in developing the new vision? Did students, directors, and other staff have a voice in the process? Was there strong buy-in from division staff and students? Second, what process was used to implement the first round of budget cuts? Were the first cuts supported by data and a thorough needs analysis? Was there a clear communication plan for the budget situation and the mandate to make cuts? Regardless of the strategies employed to reach this point, Marin will have to address three main areas going forward: communication; staff development and morale; and financial solutions.

Communication

All effective change processes require a comprehensive communication plan and a high degree of transparency. The plan must outline the constituency groups to be addressed, specify a timetable and the methods of communication to be used, and clearly state the messages to be conveyed. The most important aspect of a communication plan is listening; meetings with staff and students (individually and in groups or departments) to hear their ideas and concerns can be helpful and can raise issues and solutions that had not been considered.

Systems can be developed to provide a feedback loop that can be used in crises and in routine matters. Periodic electronic newsletters and state of the division addresses can keep staff and students apprised of issues facing the university and the division. Ad hoc committees, such as a budget crisis committee, can be used to tap the expertise of talented and creative staff. Even if everyone cannot be on the committee, everyone should have access to a source for information and feedback through peers. In situations like this, some institutions have sent out questionnaires or posted surveys online as a way for staff to recommend cuts and share ideas. This type of transparency clarifies the issues faced by the division and builds trust among those affected.

Staff Development and Morale

Given the fear engendered by repeated budget cuts, it is important to continue professional development and morale-building activities. The professional development committee must continue to provide professional and personal growth opportunities. With travel funds likely limited, the committee can draw on low-cost options such as webinars, 1-day conferences, and local experts. An on-campus conference can be organized featuring presentations that have been delivered by staff members at professional meetings. Book clubs and discussion groups are other low-cost professional development tools.

It is especially important to maintain morale during difficult times. One model to consider is the FISH! Philosophy (Lundin, Paul, Christensen, & Blanchard, 2000), a set of work/life practices created by ChartHouse to improve organizational culture. The model includes four principles: (1) be there, (2) play, (3) make their day, and (4) choose your attitude. The concepts were inspired by observing the work culture at the Pike Place Fish Market in Seattle, Washington. In addition to morale-building activities, the staff development committee can arrange recognition ceremonies and social activities. One institution hosts a division bowling social every summer. Nothing builds camaraderie like laughing and playing together, and a little friendly interdepartmental competition.

Financial Solutions

The place to start in any budget reduction is the division's priorities outlined in the vision, mission, and strategic plan; herein rest the guiding principles for difficult financial decisions. Next, consider which division units and functions are aligned with the university's broader mission and strategic plan. Performance data on student learning outcomes, progress toward goals, and the impact of objectives are all helpful in prioritizing financial decisions. This information can suggest budget-cutting options for stakeholders to consider. Cost savings can be estimated for each option, and options can be evaluated against the guiding principles. Programs or activities that are not essential to the mission can be temporarily suspended and reestablished at a later date.

Along with budget reduction strategies, a menu of new resource options should be explored during tight budget times. New sources of funding can be generated through grants and gifts; if the division does not have a fundraising plan with dedicated development staff, this is the time to invest in that area. Shifting expenses to alternative sources of funding—such as auxiliaries and student fees—may free up resources for mission-critical expenses. Evaluate whether student fees can be created, increased, or shifted to cover expenses traditionally covered by state funds. Finally, consider whether certain programs and services might work well through an outsourcing model; that is, operated and funded by a third party for a fraction of the cost.

Gain Support

Once all these options have been considered and the budget cuts are ready for implementation, the vice president should consult with the president to get support and buy-in on what might become controversial decisions. Inevitably there will be objections to the cuts; support from the president will make it less likely that the vice president's decisions will be overturned. When these decisions are confirmed, staff and students must be informed as dictated by the communication plan. Although no vice president wants to see budget cuts, it is important to convey an optimistic message: The division has been through tough times before and has survived.

Response by Arthur Sandeen, Former Vice President for Student Affairs, University of Florida

When assuming a new leadership role, it is impossible to accurately predict the challenges one might face. For many vice presidents for student affairs, financial cuts are realities of leadership positions in higher education. Although it was not discussed specifically in this case, one can assume that Marin did his due diligence to understand the financial landscape of the institution and of the division he was inheriting. Marin may or may not have had information on the differences between his leadership style and that of the former vice president for student affairs. However, what he might have discovered in the interview process would not have changed where he is now.

Marin has two main choices: resign or make things work. Resigning in the face of the insurmountable challenges might be understandable, but every leadership position includes challenges. Walking away could have negative long-term career implications; hiring committees are likely to ask references about how potential candidates responded during difficult times. Marin's other choice is to take the steps necessary to lead the division through this tumultuous time.

Remain Optimistic

Marin might be tempted to blame himself for this situation. In hindsight, he might think he should have anticipated complications related to implementing a new vision as a transitioning vice president. He may wonder why he did not ask more questions about the institution's financial status. Leaders sometimes internalize institutional failures and lose confidence in their judgment. Marin could not have predicted the challenges he encountered, and he should remain optimistic about the future. The staff needs a confident, self-assured leader as they go through this period of uncertainty. Marin must understand what he needs to handle stress in this situation. The key is to remain optimistic.

Develop a Protocol

During the first round of budget cuts, Marin applied a people-first philosophy of maintaining jobs. While this may have been appropriate for the first round, it might not work for the second round. Marin and his leadership team must establish a protocol to guide financial decision making in good and bad times. This protocol should be used to make tough decisions. Preferably, the protocol would have been developed before a crisis occurred, for use in multiple scenarios. Difficult situations are good reminders of the importance of having a sound financial philosophy.

Make the Tough Decisions

Making tough decisions is part of a vice president's job. These decisions involve people's lives, and the outcomes are not always clear; most people would rather not have to make these kinds of decisions. In the second round of budget cuts, it might be necessary to set aside the ambitious strategic plan and abandon plans to restructure the staff. Layoffs might be unavoidable. Marin cannot maintain a people-first philosophy indefinitely; at some point, basic programs and services for students cannot be reduced any further to maintain personnel. An internal sounding board—a small group of key staff members—can help Marin process tough decisions that will affect campus and division culture.

Communicate Clearly and Often

During times of change and uncertainty, it is important for the vice president to communicate clearly and often. Marin should be visible and personally invested in collecting feedback and addressing concerns; delegating those responsibilities to subordinates is not a good idea under these conditions. Even though cuts in programs or staffing levels are necessary, they can lead to anxiety in the organization; many staff members will wonder if their position is next. Clear and frequent communication is essential in transitions, especially transitions that include a crisis. The vice president should continuously share information about the university's financial condition and about the protocol used to make decisions. Be honest and transparent.

Response by Brandi Hephner LaBanc, Vice Chancellor for Student Affairs, University of Mississippi

Marin must forge ahead, but in a cautious and strategic manner. He must think about tackling this challenge on various levels. First, he must carefully push back with senior administrators as an advocate for the important work of student affairs professionals. Next, he must find his inner businessman and identify new revenue streams to replace depleted financial resources. Finally, he must work with his best asset—the employees—to find creative solutions to the challenges ahead.

Advocate for the Division

A pushback approach must be carefully and respectfully employed. As the vice president for student affairs, it is incumbent upon Marin to advocate for the division in an effort to reduce or eliminate the second round of budget cuts. This advocacy must be well prepared and highly strategic. Specifically, he should remind President Perry of her vision and her belief that student affairs could do more to advance the academic mission of the university. Marin should highlight the division's ability to make that a reality by providing specific examples of important student affairs contributions that enable academic initiatives to succeed. Examples might include student retention rates, engagement of international students, higher academic achievement of involved students, or job placement rates achieved by the campus career center. Marin should focus on student affairs services, programs, and initiatives that correlate directly with student success or that make the university an attractive option for students and families.

Because Perry and Marin have a shared vision for student affairs and the university, it may be appropriate for Marin to respectfully remind the president that she initially told him to execute a bold new vision for student affairs. It is sometimes helpful to take leadership back to key decision points and to revisit philosophies and direction that were agreed upon. Given the extreme pressure the president is under and the number of conflicting agendas, sometimes clarification of the vision can be a helpful reminder. It is Marin's obligation, on behalf of the division and students, to remind senior leadership of the importance of student affairs in the campuswide vision.

Take a Business Approach

Marin must look at the business angles of these budget cuts. First, he should calculate the cumulative impact of both budget cuts on student affairs compared with the effect on other divisions. Has every division been asked to cut the same amount in whole dollars or percentage of the total budget? Second, this budget cut is in response to a reduction in state allocations; therefore, Marin should analyze what portion of the student affairs budget is funded by state funds. For example, if the division's total state budget is $4 million, a $3 million budget cut would represent 75%. From this perspective, the budget cut could be overly detrimental to the division. Third, the impact of the budget cut on the delivery of programs and services has to be analyzed. A $3 million reduction in the state allocation could require overhaul of departments, layoffs, and reductions in essential services and programs. It could also force significant fee increases or implementation of a pay-per-use approach. Neither of these options is attractive, and both will have adverse effects on students. Finally, from a business perspective, significant budget reductions can negatively affect the public image of the university and tuition revenue (student recruitment and retention). With these business-minded analyses of the budgets cuts, Marin may be able to reduce the secondary cut or request an exception.

Marin should outline contingency plans for raising revenue and reducing expenses in a worst-case scenario. Areas to consider in seeking to raise revenue in student affairs include: offering sponsorship opportunities that could provide funding for specific departments or programs; applying for grant or foundation funding for certain departments or initiatives; soliciting a specific donor with strong connections to student affairs and a high likelihood of giving; and charging fees for services to nonstudents in units such as campus recreation and the medical clinic. On the other hand, Marin should look closely at departmental budgets and determine whether expenses can be reduced by cutting programs or eliminating duplication. Times have changed, and expenses must be prioritized on the basis of outcomes rather than traditions. Some programs will have to be eliminated and services combined. Many institutions employ hiring freezes, require bulk purchases, cap travel expenses, and hire only work-study students when expenses need to be reduced.

Communication

How Marin leads his division through this financial crisis is important. He must remain highly transparent, as there is already a high level of uncertainty and anxiety about the future. Marin can attain this transparency by communicating frequently about approaches and outcomes. He should employ multiple methods of communication: formal correspondence, meetings, newsletters, and e-mail. He should encourage staff to offer ideas and solutions in person or by e-mail. His people-first philosophy needs to be front and center; the goodwill he has gained will help him through this crisis. Sharing good *and* bad news is important; most people just want to know the truth so they can make decisions for themselves. Marin must continue to trust his gut instinct and be authentic as he leads the staff through the tumultuous times ahead.

Chapter Summary

This case reflects the complexity of the vice president for student affairs role and the impact environment and culture can have on a leader's effectiveness. At the core is a vice president who is attempting to respond to a new environment, meet the president's expectations, satisfy the needs of students, and manage staff expectations and anxieties. In an effort to establish a bold new vision, he moved faster than he normally would have; as a result, he did not garner the buy-in necessary for his team to deal with internal crisis. Massive structural changes followed by budget cuts overwhelmed the system.

- Whether or not the division is going through significant changes, a new vice president for student affairs must communicate frequently and be transparent. A new leader is a change for the division. While vice presidents might feel as though they are being redundant, people need to hear messages repeatedly. Express the brutal truth to help everyone understand the complexity of the situation. Let them know by how much the university budget is being reduced and the division's responsibility.

- Advocate for the needs of students and the organization. Understand the division's budget and funding sources. Determine whether the cuts will affect certain areas more than others, and adjust accordingly. Consider how to communicate with the president and stakeholders about the impact of proposed budget cuts. Do not hesitate to work with the president or CFO to reconsider the percentage of cuts from student affairs.

- ① Create and communicate a vision for the future. Lead the division in a direction that reflects the new funding levels. Your vision should inspire and guide the division in its efforts to meet the needs of students. An inspiring vision can reinvigorate staff and bring new energy following the stressors of change.

- ① Pursue new revenue sources to offset budget cuts. Revisit old practices to identify any opportunities to save money or increase revenue. There may be opportunities to outsource certain operations or eliminate redundancies. If student affairs has not yet started a fundraising and development program, establish one that could provide funding for important initiatives.

- ① Maintain an optimistic outlook and help others do the same. Understand that some people are experiencing fear and anxiety; acknowledge those emotions and create a safe environment for expressions of concern. During this time of change, it is important to have a strong team that comes together to solve problems. Take time to find inexpensive ways to celebrate small victories.

- ① Renegotiate expectations with the president. The president initially requested a bold new vision for student affairs, but that was before the budget crisis. Meeting those vague expectations would be a challenge even without a shortened timeline and decreasing budget. The vice president should communicate the difficulty of accomplishing this task under the current circumstances.

The role of vice president for student affairs is highly complex. The position is full of tough decisions and competing priorities; nowhere is this more apparent than during budget cuts. The vice president must remain flexible and responsive to the needs of the division and the culture of the institution. Certain problems must be approached with keen insight into the management culture of the institution. During challenging times, leadership from the vice president is crucially important for the division to accomplish its goals.

Reference

Lundin, S. C., Paul, H., Christensen, J., & Blanchard, K. (2000). *Fish! A proven way to boost morale and improve results*. New York, NY: Many Rivers Press.

Crisis Response Protocol

Amy Hecht, Johnetta Cross Brazzell, Debbie Kushibab, Gail A. DiSabatino, and Theresa A. Powell

---

Martha Jenkins is a first-time vice president for student affairs at Martin University, a private suburban institution. The president made clear that one of her first tasks would be to improve the quality of student life and address a recent increase in enrollment. While Jenkins is trying to focus on that task, several student crises arise. Crisis communication is a challenge because of departmental silos and the lack of a university police force. Jenkins realizes that the Division of Student Affairs is not prepared to effectively manage these incidents and that perhaps she has been focusing on the wrong goal.

Institutional Background

Martin University is a private, comprehensive, suburban research institution in the northeastern United States. Founded in 1887, it offers degrees in business, education, liberal arts, engineering, and nursing. Martin is well known for its cooperative education program and the high employment rate of its graduates. Martin has a diverse student body: 60% White, 14% Black, 10% Asian, 11% Hispanic, and 5% international students.

Jane Smith has been president of the university for more than 10 years. She is highly respected by the community and has accomplished a number of strategic initiatives to advance the institution. During her tenure, Martin has experienced unprecedented growth in enrollment, from 20,000 to 30,000 students. Smith has also worked to improve town-gown relationships by creating innovative business partnerships that have benefitted the university.

Overall, Martin is a relatively safe campus. Smith's predecessor dissolved the university's police department during a financial crisis and outsourced campus safety and security to the local suburban police department. This move has saved the institution millions of dollars and has resulted in a unique relationship between the university and the local police department.

Division of Student Affairs Background

The Division of Student Affairs is composed of a dean of students' office, student activities, campus recreation, counseling services, orientation office, housing and residential life, disability support services, and a career center. A majority of the staff have been at Martin University for more than 15 years. Collectively, the team of directors has a tremendous amount of organizational knowledge—they know how to get things accomplished on campus and how the politics of the institution work. However, many are not involved in national organizations or professional development opportunities, which contributed to a lack of knowledge of the broader issues facing student affairs and higher education. Many programs and services at Martin University can be described as "the way it has always been done."

For the previous 10 years, Mike Mathis led the Division of Student Affairs. Mathis was promoted internally from his position as dean of students to serve as the chief student affairs officer. He was well liked and known for his laid-back approach; however, this approach did not allow for much change. Mathis was not a strategic planner and failed to anticipate the impact 10,000 new students would have on campus life. As a result, there have been rumblings from the student body about the quality of campus life and the availability of programs and services.

When Mathis resigned to accept a vice presidency elsewhere, Smith took the opportunity to conduct a nationwide search for a vice president for student affairs. The university hired Martha Jenkins, who had previously served as dean of students at a neighboring state institution. This was Jenkins' first vice presidency, and she was excited about the opportunity. Throughout the interview process, the president and others were clear about their desire that the new vice president address improvements in student life required by the increase in enrollment.

Quality of Student Life

Jenkins spent much of her first month on the job meeting with staff, students, and other stakeholders, seeking to understand all the opportunities to improve programs and services. She focused on the quality of student life and devoted the majority of her time to that issue. Her team was open to sharing their experiences and the history of the organization. Jenkins sensed that the team would resist major changes in their work, but she knew that change would be necessary.

About a month into her new position, Jenkins received a call from a concerned parent. He said, "I am sure you know what happened last night to my son. I figured you would want to talk with me, so I thought I would call." Jenkins was embarrassed to admit that she did not know what happened. She learned that the man's son had been airlifted from campus the previous night after sustaining a head injury while skateboarding on a main campus walkway.

After promising to look into the situation, Jenkins hung up and went to speak with her dean of students, Mack Adams. Adams was not aware of the situation but was not surprised that the Division of Student Affairs had not been contacted. He responded to Jenkins' concern by saying that he was sure someone on campus was handling the situation. This did not satisfy Jenkins, who had assumed that her team would be in the loop and handling crisis situations.

Jenkins had experience managing crises in her previous positions, so she knew what steps to take. Although student affairs was not a first responder, such as the police or fire departments, she believed that the division should be notifying faculty and reaching out to students. She quickly met with the director of campus safety, Bret Daniels, who oversaw a small four-person office. As a retired police officer, Daniels had connections with the local police department and understood how it operated. He told Jenkins that communication had never been a problem before, and he did not understand the need for student affairs to receive notification. However, he promised that in the future his office would communicate better about incidents on campus.

Two months later, the local news broke a story of a Martin student killed in a car crash near campus. Neither Jenkins nor her team had been notified about the accident—they learned of the student's death on the morning news. Jenkins was furious; communication had once again lapsed, and she felt blindsided. Although the president had not specifically said that she wanted to know immediately about a student death, this had been common practice for Jenkins in her previous role.

Jenkins immediately called Daniels to gather more information. Daniels said that he had not received word from the local police and was also just learning about this accident. He was confident that the police would handle the situation. He said they were the experts and there was not much to be done by student affairs.

Jenkins had met the local police chief during her first week on the job. He seemed like a reasonable person who put student safety first. She thought she might be able to work directly with the chief to ensure that her team received information in the future. However, she was hesitant to go around the director of campus safety. Jenkins had only been at Martin

University for 6 months, and strong relationships would be essential to her success. At the same time, she knew that student affairs had to play a greater role in crisis response.

Jenkins realized that she had been too focused on one goal and needed to quickly recover. She needed to address the crisis response issue, and she wondered what else she should have focused on. She hoped that she had not learned this lesson too late.

Response by Johnetta Cross Brazzell, Former Vice President for Student Affairs, University of Arkansas

Jenkins is not focused on the wrong goal. The quality of campus life, the increase in enrollment, and campus safety are intertwined and should be approached that way. All three elements should be tied together and presented that way to the greater campus community.

Redefine the Quality of Campus Life

Even as Jenkins addresses the crisis, she must start having redefining conversations with her vice presidential colleagues, especially the provost or chief academic officer and her student affairs staff. She must enlist the support of all the vice presidents, emphasizing their vested interest in developing a holistic approach to improving the quality of campus life. They should understand the benefits of such an approach and the negative consequences of not working together to develop one.

For her staff, Jenkins must define a student affairs philosophy centered on improving the quality of campus life. Such a focus will probably reshape staff roles. To reduce anxiety and resistance, Jenkins should include staff in the process of redefinition. The division's budget should include funds for staff to attend national organization meetings, where they will be exposed to professional development opportunities. To help facilitate this conversation, Jenkins should bring in a couple of external consultants.

Focus on Campus Safety

The campus safety issue requires immediate attention. Jenkins and her staff must be in the loop concerning student safety episodes. To whom does the director of campus safety report? Jenkins needs that vice president as an ally, and she needs to have the director of campus safety on the same page with her about how the campus should receive information about student incidents from the local police department. If she meets resistance at any level, Jenkins should involve the president. This issue is too important to let slide; the potential exists for legal liabilities if the campus continues to be late in hearing about and responding to student safety incidents.

Enlist the President

At all times, Jenkins needs to keep the president informed about her assessment of campus life and her plans for moving forward. When appropriate, she should enlist the president's involvement. Once Jenkins, Daniels, and Daniels' supervisor agree on an approach to the local police department, Smith should take the lead in approaching the city.

Response by Debbie Kushibab, Vice President for Student Affairs, Estrella Mountain Community College

Institutional fit is crucial to the success and enjoyment of student affairs work. For instance, a student affairs officer who has only worked for large research universities may have a difficult time adjusting to the mission of a small rural community college. While the work is the same, the student populations and challenges are different.

Just as important in a senior administrator's decision to accept a new job is position fit. A leader might be moving from one large university to another, but the position might be totally different in organizational structure, budget, staff, and roles of the chief student affairs officer. A leader should not make any assumptions when considering a position at a new college.

Clarify Expectations

Vice presidential candidates should take the time to create a list of expectations of the role and purpose of the position. This will enable candidates to have a productive conversation with the president during a second interview. Some administrators might think certain things are a no-brainer, like student affairs being informed of student crises. Candidates should add everything they can think of to the list, and then ask the president about his or her expectations for the position. This is a negotiation, and some issues can be resolved at this point. If some things cannot be changed or are considered to be nonnegotiable, at least the candidate can make an informed decision about the position.

Understand Current Issues

Along with any direction and vision that a vice president receives from the president, the vice president will also want to know about all current issues. This is the stuff a candidate will not read about on the institution's website or in the annual report. Candidates will want to know if any employees in the division are being disciplined, if there are any budget problems, and who is not speaking to whom.

While it is best to start with no surprises, that is probably unlikely. No matter how much research the successful candidate conducted to prepare for interviews, they will not discover everything. A candidate must decide what is most important to them in the role as chief student affairs officer, and determine whether both the position and the institution are a fit.

Do Not Assume That All Roles Are Similar

In this scenario, Jenkins spends her first few months focused on the quality of student life. She talks with students, staff, and the community. This takes time, but it is time well spent when it comes to formulating the division plan. Her misstep was assuming that her new position would be the same as her previous position. She did not understand that the role of the chief student affairs officer at this university did not include handling student crises. She was furious with the director of campus safety for not communicating with her, and her anger probably confused him.

A better approach would have been to discuss the matter with the president. In this conversation, Jenkins could ask for changes in crisis management procedures. She could describe her knowledge and experience with crisis communication and management, and the role she played at her former institution. The president might not be familiar with the role of student affairs in dealing with situations that could have severe consequences to the institution if they are not handled properly. Jenkins could describe how a crisis prevention and intervention plan could supplement the efforts she is making to improve the quality of student life at Martin University.

Response by Gail A. DiSabatino, Vice President for Student Affairs, Clemson University

This case covers an issue that is not uncommon for new vice presidents: An institution does not always recognize its needs, and it takes a lot of probing to uncover hidden weaknesses or potential for crisis. Jenkins is not alone in discovering new challenges as the layers are peeled back. In starting a new position, it is important to seek to understand the culture and listen to stakeholders. Jenkins did the right thing by listening and learning before making any significant changes or introducing new initiatives. Through her communication efforts, she was able to prioritize improving the quality of student life as an important goal for Martin University's growing population.

Despite one's best efforts to gather as much information as possible, sometimes the only way to figure out what you do not know is to fall into it. I experienced some very similar situations in a position where housing was not a part of student affairs, and the school did not see the need to involve us in on-campus critical incidents. The police seemed to interact with student affairs staff only during office hours. It took patience to change the situation, and Jenkins should be prepared to tap into hers and to focus on building a culture of trust and transparency.

Use the Opportunity to Educate

Jenkins should remain confident that she has the experience necessary to navigate this situation and help the university better manage crises. The police chief and director of security may have good intentions and believe they have it covered. However, they do not know what they do not know. The vice president's job is to leave her ego at the door, allow others to gain confidence in what she has to offer, and get them to buy into why they need to collaborate with student affairs and other divisions to establish clear and broad protocols for dealing with critical incidents and crises. Providing examples of how she has dealt with parents and alumni in previous complex situations could help people understand the potential value of her collaboration.

Develop Your Staff

Jenkins should work closely with the dean of students, Mack Adams, to learn how critical incidents have been managed in the past and the role he played. He may or may not be comfortable with the current state of affairs. He may have wanted to take on more responsibility but did not know how to serve as a crisis manager. Jenkins should assess the dean's skill set, his perception of his role, and his interest or lack of interest in expanding his role. She will need Adams to play an active role moving forward.

Build Strategic Relationships

Jenkins should take the security director to lunch so they can get to know each other. She should describe her previous positions and the role she played in supporting students and families during difficult times. Jenkins should invite the security director to join a team that she will pull together to look at how the university and the community can best serve students during these times. She should ask him who he thinks should be at the table. If he does not mention the police chief, she should be sure to let him know that she will be inviting the chief to participate in the discussion.

Jenkins should make a list of the functions that student affairs can and should perform in dealing with critical incidents and crises. The list does not have to be all-inclusive, but it should be clear enough that Adams, Daniels, and the police chief can see how central these activities are to student care, success, and development.

Jenkins should be sure to let the president know how concerned she is about the current state of affairs and why it needs to change. If she mentions the legal and public relations liabilities of not having a thoughtful and comprehensive plan, she will certainly get the president's attention and likely receive the support she needs. The president may also be interested in knowing how critical incident and crisis management are tied to enrollment and the overall student life enhancements she asked Jenkins to tackle. Jenkins should tell the president that she is reaching out to the police chief and the director of security, as well as the director of public affairs, general counsel, and appropriate academic administrators. The president will appreciate being made aware of the concern and the fact that Jenkins has a plan to deal with it. The president may be able to provide some insights into how things have worked in the past, how to deal with some of the players, and where Jenkins might find support.

Once Jenkins has talked with Adams, Daniels, the police chief, and Smith, she will be ready to bring the other players to the table. She may want to start with an invitation to a dialog or a webinar on crisis management followed by discussion. If this kind of universitywide conversation about crisis management has not occurred before, it is likely that many people will be grateful for being included. They have probably seen the need but did not know how to go about addressing it.

Response by Theresa A. Powell, Vice President for Student Affairs, Temple University

A vice president will always be solving problems. The objective of problem solving is to find a better solution, not the perfect solution, because no such solution exists. The approach to every situation or scenario is contingent upon the institution, the parties involved, the administration in charge, and the community and campus climate, as well as the short- and long-term goals of the university. And just as there are multiple solutions to various problems, there are also multiple problems unique to various universities. Unfortunately, we do not have the luxury of focusing on one problem at a time, seeing it through to resolution, and moving on to the next one. Like a juggler, we have several balls in the air at any given time. And, as any vice president knows, sometimes these balls seem like knives or flaming torches. Incoming executives should prepare in advance to manage the myriad issues they will face. They should not wait until Day 1 on the job to learn about reporting structures, staff expectations, crisis protocol, and so on. They must be familiar with current operating systems in advance. The best advice I can offer a new vice president is do your homework.

Confronting an Ineffective Practice

In this scenario, a new vice president is facing a common problem: lack of communication among departments. This is not necessarily deliberate; it may simply be the result of years of status quo. Often, when a new staff member joins an institution, he or she can see things with a fresh perspective, in which the status quo seems misguided or inefficient.

The new vice president may have strong ideas that have proved effective elsewhere, but she might not want to come charging out of the gate. She may see possibilities for connections and collegiality, but she might also sense hostilities or resistance to suggestions for change. A new vice president may wish to simply implement a new structure, but without buy-in from all or the majority of involved parties, she could be wasting time, energy, and resources. And finally, while she is tackling a particular problem, what other situations might be suffering from lack of attention? If the new vice president focuses on a single problem for a significant period, what other issues might fall through the cracks?

Before the job starts, the new vice president should research the institution as comprehensively as possible. More research might have yielded the information about crisis management that came as a shock to Jenkins. During her interviews, she could have addressed this lapse and stated her expectation that the Division of Student Affairs would be involved in all student incidents. Unfortunately, once a vice president has been on the job for a while, there will be too much going on to focus on a single problem; spending time and energy on one issue will not be realistic.

Planning and Prioritizing Goals and Initiatives

If the vice president has neglected to do her research and clarify her expectations during the interview process, she is likely to find herself in the position described in this case study. She has already been working for several months, but at this point she needs to stop, take a deep breath, and reassess. Reassessment is a critical component of effective organization and action. Jenkins should start by listing all outstanding issues and concerns that require action. This is not an exhaustive list of every imaginable concern; it is a list of items that require direct action in the immediate future. Then she should prioritize the items. She should seize any opportunities to delegate; delegation will free up her own agenda and provide opportunities for mid- and senior-level staff to exercise leadership and gain experience.

Before Day 1, the vice president should have met with staff members, at the very least with her leadership team. During these initial meetings, she should have prepared her new staff for impending changes. The president conducted a national search for a new leader, so no one should be surprised to hear that changes will be made to help the division function better. One change is the policy toward professional development—the new vice president needs to clarify that involvement with national organizations and professional development opportunities is not optional, it is expected. At the same time, she should ask her staff, "What are your expectations for me?" In this case study, Jenkins has spent a month meeting with her staff. I would suggest more meetings. This time should be spent not just talking, but listening—really listening—so she can triangulate and make informed decisions about what the division is doing well and what items require attention. She should ask critical questions, as the quality

professional involvement

216

of her questions will affect the way she is perceived. Asking critical questions will enable Jenkins to portray herself as a strategic thinker rather than simply an information gatherer.

Acting on a Major Initiative

One of the items on the list of priorities will be crisis management response. The quality of student life is affected by crises and crisis response. Jenkins has already devoted considerable time to this issue, but much of this time has not been spent effectively.

There are several roads she can take to address this issue. A crisis response protocol needs to be enacted at a high level and should involve all relevant parties (e.g., campus safety, communications, student affairs). When these parties meet to discuss the protocol, Jenkins can praise the work that has already been done and concentrate on building a team that is inclusive, collaborative, and collegial. This is the time for her to use her influence, not her power or authority. Devising a protocol could be a small and quickly realized goal, or it could require considerable time and effort. Because the issue affects multiple parties, the old system is firmly established, and the vice president is still fairly new, a task force might be the way to go. A task force involves representatives from all affected parties; asks for contributions and ideas from everyone on the committee; and yields a product that is collective. People get behind what they help create. The task force can use benchmarking data from peer institutions so that everyone can see the possibilities for success with alternative models.

In this case study, the vice president is playing catch-up. Ideally, she would have laid out her expectations for a crisis response protocol in her initial meetings with the president, the chief of police, the director of campus safety, and her staff. This proactive approach would have obviated the need for a reactive response following the two incidents. At the very least, she should have followed up immediately with Bret Daniels after the first incident to make sure that a different protocol would be followed in the future. In that meeting, she should have described her vision for how future incidents would play out. Interpersonal relations can be tricky, but they should not be avoided or tiptoed around. A vice president has to have strong working relationships and clear expectations of her staff as well as her colleagues.

If the vice president attempts to implement a new reporting structure too long after taking office, she can expect to encounter a number of impediments to her progress. If she attempts to correct the crisis management response protocol unilaterally, she might face significant resistance and a lack of cooperation, if not outright ill will. However, if she acts proactively, works collegially, and asks for help from campus and community partners, her chances of creating a successful collaborative model are good. And while focusing on this issue, she should simultaneously keep her eye on other relevant issues, using her colleagues' expertise and availability to her advantage by making specific staff members responsible for these ancillary issues. If she has already gotten off on the wrong foot, she may face challenges, but they will not be insurmountable. Although she may have to play catch-up, she can rebound and refocus. Dwelling on our mistakes is not productive; we learn and develop from our missteps and use the knowledge gained as an opportunity for growth.

Chapter Summary

In this case study, Vice President Martha Jenkins made assumptions about the expectations for her new role. She focused on making strategic changes but did not examine areas in which processes needed to be developed, such as crisis response. Jenkins did not clarify procedures, such as emergency notifications, and relied too heavily on her experience. Making the assumption that a new institution handles issues the same way your previous institution did can get you into trouble. Past experiences get vice presidents hired, but quickly adapting to the new environment will keep them employed.

> ① One significant difference between past and current experience is the culture of the organization. Culture influences the way people operate. As a new leader, it is important to understand the

new culture. Often those within a culture are not even aware of the nuances, so new members of the organization have to learn the culture through experience. However, by asking critical questions and observing behaviors, a new leader can pick up important clues about the organization's culture.

☝ It may be appropriate to clarify roles and expectations, especially if you see discrepancies between position descriptions and information you receive verbally. First, take your supervisor's style into account. If the president or provost tends to have a hands-off style, trying to involve him or her with details may not be the best course of action. However, discussing expectations with the president or provost can help you be successful. Even if you have been successful in this role at another institution, it is important to understand that expectations may be different in your new position.

☝ Redefine the role student affairs can play in crisis response, as well as the impact crises can have on the overall quality of student life. Through conversations like these, the vice president can understand more about the expectations of his or her role and express the necessity for student affairs involvement in crisis management. The vice president can paint a picture of a high-quality student life program and help others understand the importance of a comprehensive response to critical incidents involving students. These conversations can educate the campus community and help advocate for the needs of students.

☝ The vice president should build relationships with key players; in this case, the director of campus safety and the local police department. Through the relationship-building process, the vice president can share past experiences and knowledge that will increase understanding and respect for his or her role. Use these meetings to listen and try to understand the culture of the institution. Relationship-building is essential to a vice president's success.

This case study shows that it can be easy to rely on past experiences and assumptions. It is important to ensure that expectations are clear, regardless of how comfortable you may be in the position. Often, the unspoken ways of doing things are not apparent until a crisis situation arises. The better you understand your new culture, the more likely you will be to anticipate how the organization will respond to any given situation. Do not become so focused on accomplishing one task that you ignore the larger picture. As vice president, you should remain confident of your ability but also respect the new culture and be intentional about the transition.

Your Boss Is Your Predecessor

Tyjuan A. Lee, Valarie J. Evans,
Daryl L. Minus, and Kenneth Ray, Jr.

Carlos Santiago is the new vice president for student affairs at Patton University. He was not the president's first choice for the position. In addition, the president, Bertram Knight, held the vice president for student affairs position for 15 years and maintains informal relationships with a number of student affairs staff members, which undermines Santiago's authority. Santiago has begun making changes in the division. Some people in the university applaud these changes, and he is developing positive relationships with various faculty members and with the Division of Academic Affairs. However, three members of his own executive team are unhappy enough to leave, and the president has begun to treat him in an adversarial manner.

Institutional Background

Patton University is located in a large metropolitan city. The university is surrounded by housing projects, new homes, and an industrial park, making it a unique environment in which to learn and work. Patton has a student population of 60,000; the students come from more than 100 nations, but the majority (70%) are White and from different parts of the United States. The annual budget is more than $200 million, with an endowment of more than $5 million. The campus has 7 administrative buildings, a school of law, 10 residence halls, and 2 student unions.

Knight's Search for a Vice President

Bertram Knight has served as Patton University's president for 3 years; previously, he was vice president for student affairs for 15 years. The Division of Student Affairs includes the following areas: admissions and registration, counseling, academic advising, assessment, veteran's affairs, health center, student discipline, student clubs and organizations, and dining hall services. The college went through a reorganization within the first 2 years of Knight's presidency, and athletics was realigned to report to the president. When Knight became president, he tapped a colleague from another institution to serve as interim vice president for student affairs. The interim vice president was near retirement and, thus, not interested in applying for the position; he served for 2 years.

After 2 years, Knight announced that he was filling three key positions: vice president for academic affairs, athletic director, and vice president for student affairs. These three positions would be the first appointments under his administration, so it was important that the hiring process be followed to the letter. Knight expressed his expectations for these positions to Pearl Barcard, vice president for human resources, and told her that he had a candidate in mind for the student affairs position.

Barcard proceeded with the process and waited for further direction from the president. A few weeks passed and Knight informed Barcard that he had advised his friend to apply for the vice president for student affairs position. Barcard noted the name of the person and continued with the hiring process. Filling all three positions took several weeks; Knight wanted to seem unbiased and to participate only during the final selection of the candidates, but he requested frequent updates from Barcard regarding the candidates.

Once finalists were chosen, Barcard had disappointing news for the president: Knight's candidate was not selected as one of the two finalists. The president was displeased and wanted to know who was on the committee and why his friend had not been advanced. After Barcard carefully explained the human resources implications of Knight's attempt to influence the process, the president reluctantly agreed to interview the two finalists. One was a Black female from a 2-year institution; the other was a Hispanic male from a school similar in size to Patton University. The president selected Carlos Santiago, a 38-year-old gay male with two children and a partner whom he had recently wed. Santiago had 1 month to relocate his family to assume his new role as vice president for student affairs. He had served as dean of student affairs at a small liberal arts college in New England for 8 years.

Early Red Flags

Santiago had one major task before his first day on the job: to hire an administrative assistant. The previous administrative assistant retired soon after Knight was promoted to president. Santiago chose Lynn Carter, a young Black female who had recently received her associate of arts degree from the local community college. Santiago wanted an administrative assistant who was organized and a critical thinker, who could anticipate his needs, and who had a sense of humor. Carter possessed all these qualities. The two would become a dynamic duo on campus, and the division flourished under Santiago's leadership.

After a couple months on the job, Santiago was making progress within the division; however, he had observed some personnel matters that needed to be addressed. One issue involved the dean of enrollment management, who was the daughter of a friend of the president. She was consistently tardy to meetings, did not meet deadlines on assignments, and was not responsive to Santiago when he assigned tasks to her. Her staff did not respect her and often complained about her lack of leadership. Santiago spoke with the president about this matter, and Knight told him to handle it. Santiago began progressive discipline proceedings with human resources, only to be stalled near the end of the process, when Knight informed him that the dean of enrollment management would now report to the president. This was a shock to Santiago, as he was under the impression that "handle it" meant following the proper protocol to eventually relieve the dean of her responsibilities. Instead, she was now his peer.

Santiago soon encountered other issues in the division that raised red flags. First, none of the division procedures were documented. Many of the processes staff used were antiquated and created unnecessary barriers for students. Second, there was a lack of accountability among staff, who were habitually late to work and unresponsive to student e-mails. Finally, poor customer service was the rule rather than the exception. Santiago could not believe the issues he uncovered during his first 3 months at Patton.

Proceed with Caution

The university had recently implemented a new strategic plan; Santiago used this opportunity to start addressing issues in his division. Over a fairly short time, three of his deans resigned to seek other professional opportunities. In their place, Santiago hired three new deans who understood his vision and were willing to help him move the division to the next level. Santiago initiated institutionwide conversations about student success, as well as two major partnerships with the Division of Academic Affairs.

One day, while Santiago was having lunch in the dining hall, a faculty member asked if she could join him. First, she congratulated him on the many changes he had made during his short time at the institution. Santiago thanked her for the compliment and said, "I have a good team in place—I am just the voice for the division."

"No, you are more than a voice," she said. "You are transforming Patton into a more student-centered institution. This was not the case before you arrived." This comment piqued Santiago's interest and he asked her to explain. She said that for many years, student affairs just went about its business as usual, with no institutionwide conversations or partnerships with other divisions. In her opinion, Knight was so busy trying to become president of the university that he forgot about his primary role: supporting students.

At home that evening, Santiago told his partner, John, about the conversation. John listened intently and told Santiago that he needed to remember that his new boss was also his predecessor. He needed to move carefully as he created dynamic new programs and services, because he did not want to make his boss look bad. Santiago was not sure what John meant, but soon it all made sense.

The president's weekly cabinet meeting includes a roundtable discussion during which each area provides an update. Santiago was handing out his updates when the president commented, "We are out of time and will not be able to hear Santiago's updates." Santiago checked his watch and saw that 10 minutes remained. The president said, "We already know what is going on in student affairs, because I continue to receive complaints from students regarding the poor customer service." Santiago was shocked by this comment, because the president had never mentioned this to him in their weekly meetings.

After the meeting, Richard Stanley, a vice president who was hired around the same time as Santiago, came into his office and asked, "How are you doing?" Santiago replied, "I am okay." Stanley wanted to know about the president's comment during the meeting, but Santiago was unable to explain it. Stanley said "Well, it is obvious that Knight is still in this position, because you cannot even provide updates without him giving his point of view."

At his next meeting with the president, Santiago asked for clarification of his comment; specifically, examples of complaints. Knight responded, "I sent the e-mail complaints to the respective area deans to handle." Santiago requested that in the future the president include him in any communications he might have with the vice president's direct reports. Santiago also informed his team, "If anyone receives an e-mail from President Knight, please include me in your response to the president."

Knight was one of those presidents who often walked across campus. He especially liked stopping by the student center to visit former colleagues.

On one occasion, Santiago was alerted that the president had just left the assessment center and was upset with something he had heard from a staff member. Santiago waited for the president to call him, but the call never came. It was not until the next cabinet meeting that the president informed Santiago of issues in the assessment center. Santiago thanked him for the information and said, "I will follow up on it immediately." He asked that if the president had any concerns about his division, he contact Santiago immediately, so he could take action. The president turned red and said, "I will inform you of issues when I feel it is appropriate."

After this encounter, Santiago knew this was not going to be a healthy work environment for him. He sought counsel from peers outside the institution on how to handle this complicated situation.

Response by Valarie J. Evans, Vice President for Student Learning, Development, and Support, Durham Technical Community College

Santiago is wise to recognize that this is not a healthy situation, professionally or personally. He does not want to make his president look bad. What should he do? As he contemplates his next steps, he should ask himself how committed he feels to the institution, its mission, and its vision, and whether he is willing to make a personal investment to work through this difficult situation.

Knight's behavior is not the professional behavior one would expect from a university president. Ultimately, everything on campus comes under the president's purview, but Knight could have approached this situation differently. The fact that colleagues/staff from his former division still share the details of problems with him, as well as his decision not to discuss these issues directly and immediately with the current vice president for student affairs, reflects a significant problem in the administrative ranks. He seems unable to relinquish tasks related to his former position and focus on the responsibilities inherent in the presidency. Is this case study about a president who is overstepping and micromanaging or a vice president who should pay more attention to his department?

Santiago's Options

Santiago has four options for handling this situation. First, he could pull back from interacting with the president. However, this will enable the president to marginalize him and the position, and will probably leave him paralyzed in decision making. Second, he could choose to continue to work on initiatives that are important to him, to make the changes he believes in, and to hear about student affairs issues from the president. Third, he could try to develop a more positive and trusting relationship with the president and with the student affairs staff. Once trust is established, the president might be more willing to cede the necessary authority over his division and the staff might start bringing issues to him instead of informing the president. Fourth, he could start looking for another job.

Before he can deal with the situation, Santiago has to change his self-talk to emphasize the things he has accomplished and develop a clear understanding of which things he can control. He should play his successes back through his head like a chant, stand up, and break through the paralysis. Allow a day to pity himself, then develop a strategy to get back in the game.

Santiago also has to assess the external situation. Why are staff members reporting problems to the president rather than directly to their supervisor? Are they resisting new leadership or are they uncertain about how their problems will be received and acted upon? Does the president walk through student affairs more than Santiago does? Has Santiago established enough regular checkpoints to stay current with what is going on in his division? To answer these questions, Santiago has to open lines of communication. If there is something he can do to regain authority as vice president, he should find out what it is and do it. He should step back from the situation and reflect on the circumstances, his own behavior, the president's behavior, and the behavior of his staff. Reflect on the management culture and environment of the institution. Interview staff members individually and in unit groups, and work with them to build a better foundation for relationships. Plan a retreat, do some team building, and acknowledge their work. These kinds of activities will make a difference in whether or not Santiago will be successful in his transition to the vice presidency.

Establish a Joint Vision

Santiago may have erred by not bringing the staff onboard with his new vision and not being sensitive to the fact that the previous direction was set by his boss, President Knight. Although it might be an ego boost to arrive at a new institution and develop a grand vision, it is important to make sure staff understand and share the vision, and that they are willing to implement the new ideas. If the agenda is all Santiago's, it is destined to fail. The staff must be able to contribute to the plan and feel involved. Santiago must solicit their opinions and discuss implementation procedures. He should remember who established the previous vision for the division: Anything he criticizes or changes drastically can be perceived as a judgment of Knight's work. Santiago must traverse carefully around the previous strategic plan and the implementation of his own plan.

Cues From the President

At the end of the day, Santiago must adjust to the president. He has to get to know him and figure out who his trusted allies are. He must look for alliances and informal leaders on campus and in the division, learn how to work with or around these people, and decide which battles to fight. Santiago should re-evaluate his initial steps at the institution and try to determine where he went wrong. He can learn which behaviors the president values by watching other members of the leadership team, listening to how the president responds to news, and seeing what the president rewards.

Santiago has made progress since he arrived at Patton. If he intends to stay, he has to build trust with members of his staff and close the gap between himself and the president. He has to be able to rally his team around a shared vision and make sure the implementation is never more important than the people. He has to identify the sacred cows—hands-off items the president values—and work to maintain them. A new vice president for student affairs must always be willing to listen, receive constructive feedback, and build alliances.

Response by Daryl L. Minus, Executive Vice President, Learning and Student Success, Craven Community College

In college and university environments, senior-level administrators who ascend into leadership roles after overseeing other divisions in the same institution can position themselves for eventual success or immediate challenges. After serving 15 years as vice president for student affairs at Patton University, Knight assumed the university presidency. However, Knight has made decisions and taken actions that have undercut the effectiveness of his newly hired vice president. Knight's actions may ultimately undermine his tenure as president; meanwhile, for Santiago, his uncomfortable relationship with the president makes it difficult for him to effectively lead the division and function as vice president for student affairs.

Organizational Culture

Santiago's predicament is directly linked to organizational culture. Knight's long tenure as vice president for student affairs and 2 years of nontransformative leadership by the interim vice president have contributed to the evolution of a division that is deeply rooted in dysfunctional practices, beliefs, and values. Santiago feels pressure to improve systems and operations, but Knight has undermined his authority. One component of the situation is Knight's relentless focus on gaining the presidency when he was vice president for student affairs. Ambition is a common trait among executives; leaders tend to exude confidence, focus on results, and balance professional aspirations. However, untempered ambition can become self-destructive.

Knight's defects as a leader are reflected in the lack of accountability throughout his former division, his lack of adherence to the chain of command, and his impulsive decision to remove the dean of enrollment management from Santiago's reporting structure. These are not isolated incidents; they represent the apathy and ineffectiveness that have taken root and become operational norms in student affairs.

Santiago and his team of newly hired deans have transformed student affairs operations and gained respect from people in other areas at the university. However, when leaders implement transformative strategies, they should not be surprised if they get lukewarm responses from some stakeholders, especially in cases where their boss is their predecessor. Entrenched institution-centered culture and practice have dominated operations in Patton University's student affairs departments for a long time. Institution-centered perspectives are focused on protecting underperforming systems and employees, tolerating inefficiencies, and minimizing accountability. Knight is a proponent of the institution-centered focus; he is willing to maintain cultural norms and overlook organizational stagnation. For Santiago, the organizational culture challenges facing student affairs are compounded by the fact that his boss is his predecessor. Knight wanted to hire a friend for the position; anyone else who was hired would have faced excessive scrutiny.

Navigation Tools

In most cases, leaders in Knight's situation can leverage their knowledge of institutional history and their established relationships to make continuous improvements that eventually transform the institution. To do this, however, Knight would have to cultivate his role as a mentor, focusing on the professional growth and empowerment of others. Unfortunately, Knight cannot seem to let go of his role as past leader of the Division of Student Affairs. Santiago needs to be strategic about how he navigates the situation.

Communication matters. Leaders who are new to executive management roles are sure to encounter unexpected challenges. When the boss is one's predecessor, it is imperative to create effective communication channels. Santiago is already leading a renaissance in the division that is being recognized by faculty and staff across the university; it is important for him to reframe the narrative related to these accomplishments. Initiatives in student affairs can be framed as working components of the president's mission and strategic plan. This approach will create avenues for Santiago to communicate connecting points between the president's accomplishments and his own accomplishments as vice president for student affairs. In university meetings, forums, and presentations, Santiago and his leadership team can communicate organizational improvements in the division in ways that speak clearly in support of institutional success and connect to the president's vision. This approach can diminish some of the ill will manifested by a predecessor.

Expanding the narrative in this fashion can help minimize perceptions of competition and conflict in the relationship between Santiago and Knight. The president may always consider Santiago an adversary just because he was not Knight's initial choice for the position. However, the more the student affairs narrative portrays Knight as an ally in the division's transformative processes, the more likely he will be to relinquish his grip on the division and trust Santiago. This is a challenging space to operate in: Santiago will have to soft-pedal his differences from Knight and yet avoid making any decisions that could cause student affairs to revert to its previous ineffectiveness.

Cultivate and stand on your core values. Santiago has to remain true to the values that fuel his motivation to advance the division and the university. Self-reflection and personal evaluation are important. Santiago should focus on identifying his core values: beliefs, motivations, character attributes, work values, and nonnegotiables. In his attempt to find common ground with the president, he might be tempted to compromise his core values; if he does that, he will run the risk of being lulled into the same stagnation that plagued the division in the past.

Strategic exit. Santiago has to decide whether he will continue working for Knight if the situation does not improve. If leaving is a possibility, he needs to develop an action plan for a strategic exit. He should begin investigating other employment opportunities that align with his current professional trajectory. Having a plan does not mean changing work habits, losing perspective on his core values, or not supporting the work of his staff. However, Santiago has to focus on building his leadership portfolio in ways that will position him for career advancement in the event he has to leave Patton University. If he does leave, he should do so without emphasizing his differences with Knight. Leaving with class is just as important as arriving with class. Public comments that disparage a sitting president come off as unprofessional whining.

Response by Kenneth Ray, Jr., Vice President, Student Services and Enrollment Management, Hillsborough Community College

Poor relationships, micromanagement, and oversized egos are the foundation for the challenges presented in this case study. Santiago is confused and conflicted by the lack of support and the adversarial relationship with his president. He began his new position with visions of improvement and transformation, but he has discovered that it is nearly impossible to move forward without the president's support. Knight's support is lacking on two levels: (1) Santiago was not the president's preferred candidate, and (2) Knight has not completely transitioned from his previous position as vice president for student affairs.

The president's succession plan was foiled. He attempted to hire a friend as vice president—perhaps someone he trusted and considered nonthreatening. The preferred candidate would have probably been a better fit for the president and probably would have related better with the existing management staff in student affairs. Complicating matters further for Santiago is that the president appears to be using the student affairs management staff as part of his unofficial support staff in his role as university president. In addition, Santiago's positive relationship with academic affairs and some faculty may have contributed to the president's adverse behavior toward him during cabinet meetings. Watching his new vice president gain recognition and faculty approval might be causing the president to feel uneasy about his own position.

Planning Is the Key to Survival

Santiago needs to determine whether his concerns about the president's behavior are accurate. In *Working for You Isn't Working For Me: The Ultimate Guide to Managing Your Boss,* Katherine Crowley and Kathi Elster (2009) outlined steps you can take to improve the relationship with your boss. These steps are relevant to Santiago's situation. The first step is for Santiago to determine whether what he believes is happening is really happening. The best way for him to do this is to confide in a mentor outside the university. Next, Santiago needs to step back from the situation and realize that he is the one who must change, not the president. Regardless of the president's behavior, Santiago controls how he interacts with the president. Finally, he must not take the president's adverse behavior personally; that will only chip away at his confidence.

As vice president, Santiago serves at the pleasure of the president. If he intends to stay at Patton, he should start by reinventing himself and gaining the president's confidence. To do this, he needs to watch how respected members of the president's cabinet behave and emulate those behaviors when possible. He needs to learn how to anticipate needs of the president and stay one step ahead. Although it will not be an easy task, reinventing himself might be worth it to remain as vice president and move student affairs closer to the president's expectations. Improving the situation means communicating with the president to get to the heart of their disconnect and identifying mechanisms to move forward. They need to come up with a proactive strategy together, rather than constantly reacting to the past and getting stuck in miscommunication.

If Santiago's efforts to improve the situation are ineffective or he cannot embrace the president's vision, he should develop a withdrawal plan. There is nothing wrong with preparing for a graceful exit. Sometimes animosity between the president and a staff member is not resolvable. Leaving will avoid an adverse separation from the university and preserve a good work record. Leadership rises and falls on relationships. Without the proper relationships, it is difficult to lead and be led. Sometimes it is best to move on.

Keep the President Engaged

Because Knight served as vice president for 15 years, it is reasonable to expect that he will not support major changes in student affairs that are implemented without his input and consideration. With sensitivity to the president's seniority and history with the division, Santiago should explore the president's expectations. This will give Santiago a framework for working with staff to accomplish the president's goals. In moving toward achieving these goals, Santiago will gain the president's respect and trust. He should consult with the president to thoroughly appreciate the history and previous challenges. Santiago must keep the president informed and feeling connected to student affairs.

Santiago should have conversations with the president about expectations and goals. This will open opportunities for Santiago and Knight to talk about the future of student affairs. Envisioning the future is an essential leadership task. The goal is to move the president's thinking to the future and his legacy rather than the past. Santiago should keep the focus on the future while publicly praising the accomplishments of the past. In this way, he will be affirming the president's past achievements and enhancing Knight's legacy while strategically planning the future of student affairs.

In *The Secret: What Great Leaders Know and Do,* Ken Blanchard and Mark Miller (2009) described the importance of both results and relationships. Valuing results and relationships equally will enable Santiago to develop mutual interests with the president to promote the university. He must become familiar with Knight's values and incorporate them in all student affairs departments.

Stay Connected

Santiago should interact and maintain relationships with others at the institution, and continue to engage faculty in his activities. These connections might provide some protection from adverse treatment from the president. A visible relationship with students is equally important. Santiago should make it a priority to stay connected with all student functions.

Chapter Summary

Carlos Santiago finds himself in a complicated situation: His new boss is also his predecessor. He might have expected to be totally supported, because his boss understands the demands of his position. Instead, President Knight is threatened by Santiago's progress and has not let go of his former role as vice president for student affairs. Knight inserts himself into student affairs decisions to the point of undermining Santiago's authority. What should Santiago do in this situation?

- Santiago has to focus on building positive relationships within his division and with the president. Relationships are critical to the success of any leader, especially relationships with key stakeholders: staff members and the boss.

- Santiago's first task is to understand the culture of Patton University and of the Division of Student Affairs, especially in light of the fact that Knight led the division for 15 years. Santiago has implemented changes he thought made sense, but he neglected to evaluate how they were received. Some people, including three of his staff and the president, have reacted negatively.

- Santiago needs to be more accessible than Knight in the division and to encourage his staff and others to have informal conversations with him, as they do with the president. It is difficult for a new vice president to be out of the office during the first few months, but that is when he will connect with staff and create a reputation as an accessible leader.

- Santiago failed to communicate well with his staff and the president. Regular meetings with his team might have enabled him to avoid the current situation, in which the president gets information from his staff before he does. If Santiago makes informal communication a priority, his formal communications will be better received.

🔟 Santiago needed a transition strategy—a plan to integrate himself into the institution and division. He should have shared this plan with the president and his executive team for feedback and agreement; that way, everyone would have been on the same page about his priorities and next steps.

References

Blanchard, K., & Miller, M. (2009). *The secret: What great leaders know and do.* San Francisco, CA: Berrett-Koehler.

Crowley, K., & Elster, K. (2009). *Working for you isn't working for me: The ultimate guide to managing your boss.* New York, NY: Penguin Group.

THE AUTHORS

Johnetta Cross Brazzell is the former vice chancellor for student affairs at the University of Arkansas, where she retired in 2009. She received her BA from Spelman College in history and political science, MA from the University of Chicago in American history with an emphasis on the African American experience, and PhD from the University of Michigan in the Higher and Adult Continuing Education program. She has served as vice president for student affairs at Spelman College, associate dean of students at the University of Arizona, and assistant to the associate vice president of academic affairs/vice president for student affairs at the University of Michigan. She has served in numerous roles on a number of professional organizations and educational and community boards including the National Association of Student Personnel Administrators, Association of American Colleges and Universities, Arkansas College Personnel Association, and LeaderShape.

Ainsley Carry is vice provost for student affairs and clinical professor of educational administration at the University of Southern California. He earned a BS in food and resource economics, an MA in counselor education, and an EdD in higher education administration from the University of Florida. He also holds an MBA from Auburn University. Carry has served in college administration since 1998 at the University of Florida, Southern Methodist University, the University of Arkansas, Temple University, Auburn University, and currently the University of Southern California. His areas of research interest include business applications in college administration and collegiate social-innovation efforts.

Mary B. Coburn has been the vice president for student affairs at Florida State University (FSU) since 2003. A three-time alumna of FSU, she has a BA in sociology, an MA in counseling, and an EdD in higher education administration. Prior to her current role, Coburn served as vice president for student affairs at Tallahassee Community College, associate dean of students and director of orientation at FSU, and counselor at Bainbridge

College. In addition to serving on the faculty of FSU's Higher Education program, she is director of FSU's Hardee Center for Leadership and Ethics in Higher Education and director of the Jon C. Dalton Institute on College Student Values

Karen Warren Coleman is vice president for campus life and student services at the University of Chicago. She earned her BA in psychology from the University of Massachusetts Amherst, MA in higher education and student affairs administration from the University of Vermont, and she is currently a doctoral student at the University of Pennsylvania. She joined the University of Chicago in 2009 as associate vice president for campus life and associate dean of students, after serving in several roles over 10 years at the University of California, Berkeley. She has held student affairs positions at The George Washington University, the University of Vermont, and Hobart and William Smith Colleges. She also holds leadership roles in the American College Personnel Association and the National Association of Student Personnel Administrators.

Gail A. DiSabatino serves as the vice president for student affairs at Clemson University. She earned her BA from the University of Delaware, MA from Colorado State University, and EdD from the University of Pennsylvania. She has more than 30 years of experience in higher education administration, having held positions at the Georgia Technical Institute, California State Polytechnic University, Emerson College, the University of Nebraska–Lincoln, and Marshall University. Her areas of research interest include college student drinking behavior and academic integrity.

W. Houston Dougharty is vice president for student affairs at Grinnell College. He formerly served as dean of students at Lewis and Clark College, and associate dean at the University of Puget Sound and Iowa State University. His degrees are from Puget Sound, Western Washington University, and the University of California, Santa Barbara. He teaches in the graduate education program at Drake University. He is active in leadership positions regionally and nationally in the National Association of Student Personnel Administrators and the American College Personnel Association. He has contributed chapters to *Linking Theory to Practice: Case Studies with College Students* (Routledge, 2000), *The Advocate College Guide for LGBT Students* (Alyson Publications, 2006), and *Maybe I Should: Case Studies on Ethics for Student Affairs Professionals* (University Press of America, 2008).

Valarie J. Evans is senior vice president for student learning, development, and support at Durham Technical Community College. She earned her BA in psychology from Norfolk State University, MA in guidance and counseling from Old Dominion University, and EdD in community college leadership and educational administration from George Mason University. She has served in college administration since 1997 at Tidewater Community College and Durham Technical Community College. Her professional, personal, and research interests include discovering ways higher education can establish educational strategies to serve as interventions for underachieving students.

Susan M. Gardner has more than 15 years experience in academic and student affairs. She earned her BA in communication studies from Oakland University, MA in interpersonal and public communication from Central Michigan University, and EdD from Capella University. Her areas of interest and research include at-risk students, first-year programs, communications, gender studies, leadership, and assessment.

Amy Hecht is vice president for student affairs at The College of New Jersey. She earned her bachelor's degree from Florida State University and her master's and doctoral degrees from the University of Pennsylvania. She has served in higher education since 2001 at Alpha Chi Omega Fraternity, the University of Pennsylvania, Cabrini College, Temple University, and Auburn University. She also holds a faculty appointment at The College of New Jersey and served as an adjunct professor at Auburn University. Her areas of research interest include leadership development, organizational learning, and organizational development.

Brian O. Hemphill is the 10th president and professor at West Virginia State University. He earned his BA in organizational communication from St. Augustine's University, MS in journalism and mass communication from Iowa State University, and PhD in higher education administration from The University of Iowa. Before assuming the presidency at West Virginia State University, he served as vice president for student affairs and enrollment management and associate professor at Northern Illinois University. He has served as associate vice chancellor and dean of students at the University of Arkansas, associate dean of students at the University of North Carolina Wilmington, assistant dean of students at Cornell College, and coordinator of minority recruitment and retention at Iowa State University.

John R. Jones, III is vice chancellor for student affairs at the University of North Carolina (UNC) at Pembroke. He received a BA in applied mathematics from Appalachian State University, and an MA and PhD in higher education administration from the University of Iowa. He has held positions in college administration since 1998 at Purdue University, Indiana University–Purdue University Indianapolis, Northern Illinois University, and now UNC at Pembroke. Jones has served on the boards for the Madame Walker Urban Life Center in Indianapolis, Indiana; the Center for Academic Integrity; and the Association of Student Conduct Administration.

Kurt Keppler serves as vice chancellor for student life and enrollment at Louisiana State University. He holds a BS from the University of Wisconsin–La Crosse, and an MS and PhD from the University of Missouri. He was vice president for student affairs at Valdosta State University, associate vice president and dean of students at Georgia State University, associate dean of student affairs at Virginia Commonwealth University, and assistant director of student development at the University of Missouri. He held adjunct teaching positions at each institution and taught leadership seminars and courses in group dynamics, organizational behavior, and leadership theory. Keppler served as president of the National Association of Student Personnel Administrators from 2005–2006, and in 2007 was named a Pillar of the Profession.

Debbie Kushibab is an educator who has worked with the Maricopa Community College District for 25 years. She currently serves as the vice president for student affairs at Estrella Mountain Community College. She has held other administrative positions at GateWay Community College, Scottsdale Community College, and Phoenix College. She holds a PhD in higher education leadership from Arizona State University, an MA in organizational management from the University of Phoenix, a BA in communication from Arizona State University, and an AA from Glendale Community College. She has represented the college and district in service on the board of directors for United Blood Services and scholarship fundraising activities for the Women's Philanthropy Circle.

Brandi Hephner LaBanc is vice chancellor for student affairs and associate professor at The University of Mississippi. Originally from Ohio, she earned her undergraduate degree in accounting from the University of Akron, an MA in higher education from Kent State University, and an EdD in adult and higher education from Northern Illinois University. With more than 17 years of experience in higher education, she has worked at the University of Akron, Kent State University, Northern Illinois University, Arizona State University, University of North Carolina Wilmington, and Baldwin-Wallace University. Her research focuses on preparation of student affairs professionals and transition issues for graduate students, and she has published work related to campus crisis management.

John R. Laws serves as vice chancellor for Ivy Tech Community College. In this role, he oversees enrollment management, student life, academic advising, conduct, career services, disability support services, and more. He has worked in various areas of student affairs for more than 35 years at both public and private institutions, in addition to his current community college role. He is an active member of the National Association of

Student Personnel Administrators, having served on the Board of Directors and as the Community College Division Chair. He has presented at numerous conferences and published several articles.

Felicia J. Lee is assistant vice chancellor and chief of staff at the University of California, Berkeley. She has held senior-level positions and faculty roles at research universities and private liberal arts colleges. A certified executive coach, she consults extensively with universities, nonprofit organizations, community agencies, and business groups. Her expertise lies in executive coaching, talent management, diversity leadership development, strategic planning, and team building. She holds a PhD from the University of Southern California, an MA from Stanford University, and a BA from Colorado State University.

Tyjaun A. Lee is vice president for student services at Prince George's Community College. She is responsible for managing administrative units, programs, and student services including recruitment, enrollment, marketing, athletics, and auxiliary services operations. She completed her undergraduate and graduate education at Ohio University, where she received her EdD in educational leadership with an emphasis in higher education administration. She has been nationally recognized with awards and appointments for exceptional leadership and work with underrepresented/underprivileged students.

Daryl L. Minus is executive vice president of learning and student success at Craven Community College. He holds a BS in marketing from Hampton University, an MA in business education/higher education from New York University, and an EdD from the University of Phoenix in educational leadership. Over his 17-year career in higher education, he has developed and implemented first-year experience initiatives; facilitated successful institutional partnerships between academic and student affairs; created and redesigned student development/retention programs; provided institutional leadership for strategic enrollment management planning efforts; and implemented innovative student success programming.

Gage E. Paine is vice president for student affairs and clinical professor in educational administration at The University of Texas at Austin. She earned a BA in letters from the University of Oklahoma, a JD from Texas Tech University, and a PhD from The University of Texas at Austin. She has worked in student affairs for more than 30 years at both private and public universities, including serving as vice president at Trinity University and The University of Texas at San Antonio. She is known for innovative workshops, speeches, and presentations in leadership, creativity, and organizational culture.

Theresa A. Powell is a nationally renowned career professional with more than 30 years in higher education administration. Since 2002, she has served as vice president for student affairs at Temple University; previously, she was vice president for student affairs at Western Michigan University (1991–2002). She earned her BA from the University of Pennsylvania, MA from Texas Christian University, and EdD from The Ohio State University. She has worked as a consultant evaluator and team chair for the Accreditation Review Council for the Higher Learning Commission as well as the Ohio Board of Regents.

Kenneth Ray, Jr. is vice president for student services and enrollment management for Hillsborough Community College. He has more than 25 years of experience in the Florida College System, including 13 years at Palm Beach Community College where he worked in various higher education positions, including dean of student services, dean for educational services, acting vice president of student services, and interim campus provost. He is currently president of the National Council on Student Development.

Arthur Sandeen earned his BA from Miami University, MA in college student personnel administration from Michigan State University, and PhD in administration and higher education from Michigan State. Prior to his retirement, he served as dean of students and associate professor of higher education at Iowa State University, and vice president for student affairs and professor of higher education at the University of Florida. Sandeen has authored numerous articles and books on vital issues in student affairs, including *Critical Issues in Student Affairs: Challenges and Opportunities* (Jossey-Bass, 2006); *Enhancing Student Engagement on Campus* (University Press of America, 2003); *Making a Difference: Profiles of Outstanding Student Affairs Leaders* (NASPA, 2001); and *Improving Leadership in Student Affairs Administration* (C.C. Thomas, 2000).

Melanie V. Tucker is acting assistant vice president for student services in the Division of Student Affairs and Enrollment Management at Northern Illinois University. She earned her BA from Eastern Washington University, MA from the University of New Orleans, and a specialist degree from Southeast Missouri State University. She is a licensed counselor, with research interests in student retention, the impact of trauma on student development, and student transitions.

JoNes R. VanHecke has more than 20 years of experience as a student affairs professional. She currently serves as vice president for student life and dean of students at Gustavus Adolphus College. She earned a BA from Gustavus Adolphus College, an MA from Indiana University, and a PhD at the University of Michigan's Center for the Study of Higher and Postsecondary Education. She worked with the Wabash National Study of Liberal Arts Education research project. Her research interests include college student development, liberal arts education, and citizenship/civic engagement.

Index